Paws for History

While the pubs featured in this book were dog-friendly at the time of visiting, changes of ownership or other circumstances may mean that dogs are no longer welcome.

To ensure your dog is welcome and that the pub is open on the day you plan to visit, you are advised to phone and check before setting out. There is contact information at the end of the book.

The author and the publisher have done their best to ensure that the information in this book is accurate at the time of printing, but cannot be held responsible for errors or inaccuracies.

Readers should keep to public rights of way at all times, and the description of land, a building, a path or another feature in this book is not evidence of a right of way.

Paws
for History

35 Dog-Friendly Pubs and Walks in
Oxfordshire and the Cotswolds

Helen Peacocke

Illustrated by Sue Mynall

Photographs by the author

THE WYCHWOOD PRESS

Dedication

Let this book be dedicated to all those wonderful dog-lovers who bought a copy of *Paws Under the Table*, and spent many happy hours exploring new pubs and new walks with their canine friends.
Thanks to them several pubs, which were struggling with the recession, gained extra customers and others have accepted that dogs are now as welcome as their masters.

The great pleasure of a dog is that you may make a fool of yourself with him and not only will he not scold you, he will make a fool of himself too.
Samuel Butler (1835–1902)

Our books may be ordered from bookshops or (post free) from
The Wychwood Press, Alder House, Market Street, Charlbury, OX7 3PH
01608 811969

e-mail: orders@wychwoodpress.co.uk

All our books may be seen at www.wychwoodpress.co.uk

First published in 2010 by
The Wychwood Press
an imprint of Jon Carpenter Publishing
Alder House, Market Street, Charlbury, Oxfordshire OX7 3PH

The right of Helen Peacocke to be identified as author of this work has been asserted in accordance with the Copyright, Designs and Patents Act 1988

The right of Sue Mynall to be identified as creator of the drawings in this work has been asserted in accordance with the Copyright, Designs and Patents Act 1988

Text and Photographs © Helen Peacocke   Drawings © Sue Mynall

ISBN 978 1 902279 41 1

Printed in England by CPI Antony Rowe Ltd., Chippenham SN14 6LH

Contents

Introduction by Border Collie Pythius-Peacocke

Human beings observe history by looking at crumbling old buildings and statues, reading the past in all they can see, whereas canines like me feel its vibrations through our paws, sensing the passage of time with every step we take.

That said, I must admit that I didn't get very excited when Helen informed me that our next book was to be called *Paws for History*. I feared she would fill it with tedious facts and dates, rather than discuss the terrain on which we walked. In the end we came to a compromise. In this book I talk about the things that interest me and she speaks of the things that excite her.

What you make of these walks is really up to you. I would like to think you absorb the atmosphere of the countryside as I do and feel the many happenings haunting the layers beneath the soil on which we tread.

In chapters where Helen speaks of the Civil War, for example, use your imagination, try and visualise the landscape you travel filled with soldiers and horses, guns and swords.

When she invites you to visit a church en route, forget the artefacts and imagine the men who built it; the struggles they endured as they heaved heavy stones into place, and the countless hours it took them to carve the monuments. That way you will be bringing history to life and get far more from the walk than if you simply stood and stared, noted a few dates and then walked on.

Helen and I have been together for more than 10 years and whilst I can't say living with her is easy – it's certainly great fun. I never know from day to day what we will be doing, or where we will be going. The food is good; I get regular exercise and am probably the most knowledgeable dog in the county when it comes to pubs. I have come to know a bit about real ale too – no not its taste – its aroma. I love that glorious malty smell that wafts out of Helen's glass at times.

Actually, although I know this is boasting, perhaps it is worth mentioning that I am now a fully paid up member of CAMRA (Campaign for Real Ale), and (I believe) the only dog in the country to hold a CAMRA membership card. I am very proud of this honour, which was permitted due of my continued interest in pubs and my contribution to our first book *Paws Under the Table*.

Gosh what fun we have had since that book came out. I have been asked to join Helen at all kinds of fascinating events. I even got invited to the Woodstock Literary Festival! Now how many other border collies can boast of such an achievement? That was such fun, particularly as I was allowed to join Helen in the Green Room and then sit beside her while she gave her little talk at Harriet's Cake Shop. I also joined her when she spoke to readers at several really lovely Oxfordshire bookshops that make a real point of promoting local authors. Helen says we owe these independent shops a great deal. Given that they have all treated me with great respect and often place my book in the front window, I'll award them a couple of tail wags too.

Nothing has changed since our last book as far as the rules governing our walks go. When we enter a pub I still have to go straight under the table and stay there until the meal is over, because most pubs that allow me in have strict rules about canine behaviour.

Some publicans have their own dogs. I have learnt to respect these dogs, as they often take their role as Top Dog very seriously.

There are rules governing the walk too. I have to follow the Country Code, stay close to Helen at all times and come straight back when called even if I have discovered a glorious smell that warrants further investigation.

These are the rules I have to follow:

• Once the walk has begun I have to stay under close control at all times, most particularly when walking a

bridleway or byway, in case we meet a horse. Helen says I might frighten the horses and cause an accident and if I did she would be responsible.

• I must be on a lead or under close control when we approach farm animals too. Apparently farmers have the right to destroy any dog that injures or worries the animals.

• I must not jump over walls or rush through holes in hedges and must wait patiently while Helen closes farm gates securely once we have passed through them.

• I am not allowed to wander into areas where ground-nesting birds are nesting, particularly between March 1 and July 31, as vulnerable species such as skylarks can be easily disturbed if I don't stick to the footpath.

• I must always wait for Helen to put me on a lead when we approach a road and must never dart out into the road without her.

Rules that Helen has to follow when I am accompanying her:

• She must always keep a bottle of cold water in the car and provide me with a drink of water whenever I need one.

• She must never, EVER, shut me in the car on a warm day and leave me there while she goes shopping.

• She must strap me into my doggie safety harness whenever we go for a drive.

• She must always carry a couple of plastic bags to clear up after me if I make an unexpected toilet stop.

Abingdon
The Old Anchor Inn

The Old Anchor Inn which stands on St Helen's Wharf, Abingdon, overlooking the Thames, is not as old as its name suggests. The original building on this site was demolished at the end of the 19th century and the present building was once an almshouse. In the 1980s, this pub comprised of just one small room; indeed it's said that there was more room behind that original bar than there was in the drinking area.

It now boasts a reasonably large interior made up of several rooms, one of which is the original bar, yet the Anchor retains that comfortable companionable 'pubby' feeling which suggests beer comes first and the

---

Pythius says

The trouble with visits to Abingdon is that Auntie Liz and Helen spend too much time stopping here and there to enjoy the many old buildings we pass on the way from the car park to the pub. Just as I think we are heading for open country, they stop again and start chatting about ancient buildings and all that stuff.

The pub is fine, very welcoming; it's always good to visit the Old Anchor Inn, where dogs are welcome.

Walking through the town to get to the meadows is something I have learned to live with, but I do wish that Helen would see the world as I see it sometimes. What she simply doesn't realise is that I am closer to the pavement than she is. She might find mixing with the crowds exciting, but for me it is just feet, and more feet. The only highlight for me, when walking through the town, is our visit to Mostly Books, Stert Street, which is a lovely little independent bookshop that sells lots of books by local authors. As the kindly owners consider me a local author, I am always welcome. That's nice. They sometimes place my previous book in the window too, which makes me very proud.

As for the walk through the meadows, well what can I say except that there is lots of space for me to run and some really splendid little bays beside the river bank where I can play. Actually it is doggie paradise, though I should mention that as it's a public park Helen always makes sure she has a plastic bag with her, just in case a toilet stop is necessary.

food second. Chunky furniture, several stylish old leather chairs in the far corner and a well judged assortment of pictures on every wall, along with a red bricked bar, give it a warm homely feel.

The only snag about visiting the Old Anchor Inn, which stands in the old part of town, is that it has no car park; you have to use a public car park and then walk from the centre of town and along West St Helen's Street to reach it. That's fine by us, Pythius seldom complains about an extra walk, though naturally he is not over fond of walking through busy streets. Unfortunately some do find the walk off-putting, which has an adverse effect on trade during inclement weather. Naturally it's very busy during the summer months, when visitors can sit outside and enjoy the river view.

Pythius loves this pub; he is always given a warm welcome and asked if he would like a biscuit or bowl of water.

The food is basic pub grub, nicely cooked, comes in generous portions and is beautifully presented. Smaller servings at much reduced prices are available for pensioners. I will always remember the day Pythius and I sat next to a couple of delightful old gentlemen who were tucking into their warm lunch, and the way one said to the other: "Hey, this certainly beats putting those little boxes into the microwave, don't you think?" His companion looked up for a moment, nodded his head, and then continued to tuck into his lunch with great gusto.

Another reason why I am so fond of this pub is because the current licensees really do care about their customers and are prepared to put themselves out to ensure they are happy.

The Walk

Because the Old Anchor Inn stands alongside the Thames, and Abingdon is known as a river town, it's natural to suppose that a river walk is available the moment you leave the pub. It's not. You have to make your way back into the centre of town and then double back towards the bridge if you want to walk along the river bank. Or you can do what we usually do, which is to make our way back to the centre of town, admiring the Long Alley Almshouses dating back to the 15th century, and St Helen's Church, which dates back in parts to the 13th century as we walk.

Once in the centre of Abingdon at its Market Square, turn into Bridge Street, until you reach the Broad Face pub and notice a double waymarker pointing to a small lane that will take you to the medieval Abbey gardens, Abbey Meadow and the River Thames. Walk a little way down this lane and you will notice a small passageway on the left next to the Unicorn Theatre, which is part of the old abbey buildings. Take this passageway, bearing right when you come to a road junction and this will take you past a public car park and on to the Abbey Meadows.

At this point what you make of the walk is up to you. The meadows are large and abut the river, offering your dog loads of lovely shallow bays where it can splash about and have fun. You will notice that there is a weir on the right hand side which you can cross, to create a circular walk that will take you to the far side of the bridge, Bridge Street by the Nag's Head.

We tend to walk to the far end of the meadows by the weir and after crossing a footbridge make our way to Barton Fields, following the direc-

tions of the waymarker which points straight ahead.

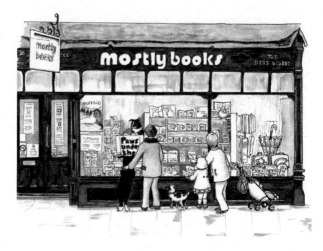

Barton Fields is a Jubilee Wildlife Space founded in 2003, which incorporates a 17-hectare wetland and meadow resource, noted for water voles, harvest mice, grass snakes and native black poplars. Great crested grebes, red kites and the occasional osprey have been sited in this area, as well as 11 species of warbler. Two small streams run through the fields and it has a riverside wood full of wildlife.

Unfortunately you can't amble at will when walking this area; a clearly marked enclosed path runs alongside one of the streams, leading you eventually to the Thames.

As this is a watery area, it tends to become very muddy during wet periods; but if you can cope with that, you will find it a delightful walk. How far you actually walk before turning back is up to you.

History

As Abingdon is thought to be the oldest town in the country that has been continuously inhabited since the Iron Age, this delightful place is steeped in history. No footnote can do justice to the many superb buildings you will find here or the stories that make up its past. There's the splendid Old County Hall in the Market Place for example, built in 1682 by Christopher Kempster, one of Christopher Wren's master builders. There's the Old Gaol built by Napoleonic prisoners of war from 1805 and 1811, and the abbey buildings.

And for those who like to know quirky things about famous people, it's worth noting that the diarist Samuel Pepys visited the Long Alley Almshouses near the Old Anchor Inn in 1668 and put some money in the alms box.

Adderbury
The Bell

We walked into The Bell in High Street, Adderbury, with confidence, having been assured that this was a dog-friendly pub by Monty, a member of the north Oxfordshire CAMRA group, with whom I had been corresponding in regards to Pythius's CAMRA membership. Monty lists The Bell among his favourite watering holes because of its friendly atmosphere and the wide choice of real ales on tap. Pythius certainly sensed he'd be made welcome as he led the way straight through the front door with that Border collie arrogance I have come to expect of him at times.

What a lovely little pub this is. Like the rest of the buildings in this picturesque village, it is constructed out of the local red maristone (ironstone).

Adderbury is thought to have been named after Eadburga of Aylesbury, a Mercian saint and princess who died in 960. Because it stands just three miles south of Banbury and is steeped in so much history, one would assume it would attract a large number of tourists. It doesn't, but that's fine by me. As far as I'm concerned its empty streets devoid of people is one of its charms.

The Bell, which is but a stone's throw from the imposing church of St Mary's, dates back to 1779, and still retains some of its original oak panelling in the lounge bar. In fact, it offers everything one dreams of finding in a rural pub including a warm and welcoming atmosphere.

Pythius marched straight for a table by the window and settled down while we decided which of the many

real ales on tap we would drink. Actually there was no contest, this is a Hook Norton pub – Auntie Liz and I both chose Hooky Gold, a pale crisp beer with a great fruity aroma, the perfect drink for a warm summer's day. We were not disappointed. There was a moment half way through our meal when Auntie Liz noted that there was an ale named Beautiful Morning listed too, which she thought we should taste, but we decided that we'd try that another day.

The Bell has a locals' bar, which is where we had our lunch. Also a lounge bar with a striking inglenook fireplace, and a music room and library which is a meeting place for the local theatre group, the bell ringers, the Morris dancers and any other village groups that fancy a get-together.

Pythius had a wonderful time, because everyone who entered the bar looked round, smiled at him and made all sorts of complimentary remarks which suggested he was a not just a nice dog, but handsome too.

The food is great, nothing fancy, but everything is cooked to order and really nicely presented. Auntie Liz went for a ploughman's plate and was most impressed, while I munched my way through a plate of battered fish and chips.

One of the great things about this pub is the way all the customers chat to each other, due in part to the friendly outgoing bar staff who go out of their way to generate friendly conversation.

We were just preparing to leave, having discussed all manner of things with the locals, including dog walks, when I heard a voice declaring that I must be Helen and the dog must be Pythius-Peacocke. I turned to discover that Monty had just entered the pub. It was one of those strange serendipitous moments that happen to us all from time to time. Although Monty had told us about the pub, we had not arranged to meet there.

Whilst chatting to the locals, Auntie Liz and I had discussed many subjects with those congregated in the bar; however we had not admitted why we were there. Monty's arrival blew our cover.

It was a fun moment, particularly as it was Monty who suggested that I register Pythius as a CAMRA member. Pythius wagged his tail on meeting him, and those kindly customers in the pub who had been advising me on Adderbury walks looked slightly bemused. It hadn't dawned on them that I'd be including this experience in a book and

---

Pythius says

The pub was great. The girls walked me towards the front door with confidence. They knew I would be welcome and I was. The food smelt good and the conversation sounded interesting, particularly when the man named Monty entered the bar and recognised me immediately (well, perhaps he noticed Helen first, but I would like to think that it was me who attracted his attention). Or maybe he spotted us at the same time, because how many times does a handsome Border collie like me sit in a pub with his mistress and an Auntie Liz? He was certainly a very friendly man.

The walk was fine. I have no idea why it was suddenly aborted – those cows looked friendly enough even though they were black and looked more like bulls than cows. Gosh what wimps the girls are. When it was decided that we would turn right rather than left, I chose to take over the walk. It was a hot day. I needed water so as it was obvious we weren't going to take the path I wanted, I marched them back to the stream.

Must admit the high spot of the walk turned out to be at the end when we discovered the stream running at the bottom of the graveyard. Gosh, that was good. Crisp, cool water in which I could run and splash to my heart's delight. What a wonderful way to finish what actually proved to be a really lovely day.

They walked and I ran for about an hour and a half before heading home. This village is riddled with footpaths, and surrounded by fields so all in all it is a dog walker's delight.

that they might be mentioned as a consequence. It proved a warm and friendly moment, such that we left wishing everyone well, whilst wondering if we should have bought Monty a drink before leaving.

The Walk

We knew that there were several walks we could have chosen, including a three-and-a-half-mile circular walk around Adderbury that crosses very pleasant undulating farmland and millstreams. (You will find a free tourist brochure in the pub that highlights this walk)

We were also tempted to take the village trail. However, on the advice of the charming young woman serving behind the bar who has two dogs of her own, we ended up doing a bit of both. She assured us that the best doggie walk, which took in two big fields and a stream, began at Croft Lane. She suggested we take that route first, then when Pythius had used up some of his energy, we could return to Adderbury and take up the village trail.

So we turned right after leaving the pub, crossed the road and headed for the lane which was but a few hundred yards along the road, just past the hairdressers. We turned down Croft Lane, which as she'd said led to a stile on the left hand side once we had passed the last house.

This stile (which is very high and not as easy to climb as one would wish) led to a field as she promised, and as she had warned, we saw those dreaded, soft gooey cow-pats scattered across the grass. There were no cows to be seen however – just palpable evidence that they had been there earlier. She'd assured us that if we did encounter cows, they would be docile, friendly beasts, so we walked on across the field to a stile we noticed in the far corner which led to another field also covered with loads of fresh fat squashy cow pats.

"Carry on," said Auntie Liz stoically. "She did say they were docile," so we did, following a very well-worn track leading towards two open metal gates – but Pythius ignored this exit, and made for the stile alongside them. It was here that we discovered a glorious little brook rippling over large rocks as it made its way between the fields. We stayed there for some time, relaxing in the shade, watching Pythius enjoy himself splashing about in the shallow water. Because it was such a fine summer's day we decided to walk on, rather than stick to the first two fields, so having crossed the brook, using the stepping stones strategically placed for easy movement, we entered a small track

through a wild area, which divided after about 10 yards. We followed it to the left and walked alongside a field of what looked like drying linseed flowers that were ready to harvest, noting as we walked that the earth was almost as red as the stones from which most of the village is built.

At the end of this track, and before we were faced with the choice of turning left and following the way sign, or continue walking the perimeter of the field by turning right, we discovered a metal kissing gate and a footpath marker.

Pythius was very positive – this was the way he wanted to go and one can't argue with a Border collie once they have made up their mind.

Perhaps we would have humoured him had it not been for several very large black bovine beasts plodding purposefully towards us. They certainly didn't look docile.

"Perhaps we should turn right," said Auntie Liz, who may be far braver than I am, but is cautious with it. "Perhaps we should," I answered as I noted those big brown-glaring eyes.

So that's what we did. Yes Pythius seemed very disappointed, but the beasts were too close for comfort. Actually he was so disappointed, he turned in high dudgeon, refusing to turn right, and set about returning the way we'd come. When a Border collie decides to organise the walk, there is not much one can do but follow. Had we continued and followed the footpath markers by turning into the field in which the cows blocked our way, we would have ended up walking one and a half miles to Bodicote, and had we wished, completed the circular walk around Adderbury.

Instead, we followed a very determined Border collie who was hell bent on returning to the stream where he could splash about and have fun.

So returning the way we had come, we met the brook again, then crossed the two fields we had originally crossed, heading for a stile we noticed straight ahead of us rather than heading left to the high stile we had originally struggled to climb. This stile led to a little lane flanked by high stone walls and eventually to the centre of the village.

Keeping the tall church steeple in our sights, we took Church Lane that leads to St Mary's, having decided to visit the church before we left.

How good that we made that decision; the church, which we reached by turning down Church Lane, proved one of the most imposing churches we had ever seen. Unfortunately the doors were locked and we couldn't gain entrance, but we could admire its many gargoyles (or were they grotesques?) who peered down on us from on high. Be assured, that this church and its large expansive graveyard is well worth making an effort to see, particularly as there's a shallow but fast running stream at the bottom of the churchyard. Turn right when you reach the small bridge over the stream and connect with a superb little footpath that eventually leaves the stream once you reach the sluice gates, taking walkers into Mill Lane and eventually the High Street and The Bell Inn.

Pythius adored the stream; it was shallow, the water was cool, and he was able to splash about to his heart's content. We definitely enjoyed this part of our walk best as it was shady, cool and picturesque.

All too soon, we arrived at the spot where we had parked the car and having treated ourselves to a cooling ginger beer from Taste Buds, Adderbury's great little butchers and fine food shop close to the pub, we made our way home.

History

Adderbury has long been noted for its Morris Dancers. Thanks to dancer Janet Heatley Blunt and publican William 'Binx' Walton, who recorded the local Morris dances during the early 1900s, the village boasts two Morris sides and celebrates a day of dance each spring. A Blue Plaque celebrating Janet Blunt's contribution to Adderbury Morris can be seen in Manor Road.

Ampney Crucis
The Crown of Crucis

L ittle did we know that on our return from Ampney Crucis, near Cirencester, we would be driving home through the daddy of all storms. But that's another story. The sun was shining when we set out for this delightful little Cotswold village close to Cirencester, reached off the B4425 Bibury road north of the town.

We phoned The Crown of Crucis, a 16th century inn that stands besides the Ampney Brook and overlooks the village cricket green, to ask if Pythius would be welcome and received the answer that we wanted to hear. Dogs were more than welcome to join their masters in the bar area if they were well behaved and prepared to place their paws under the table.

As the car had just been serviced and no longer made strange bumping noises when going into low gear, the journey there proved both comfortable and easy.

The Crown of Crucis stands on the B4425, and there's ample room for cars in its large car park. It's a large imposing hotel which has been run by the same owners for more than 20 years. As dogs are accepted as residents in certain rooms, they are also welcome in the bar area.

The main bar was buzzing with activity when we arrived. This is

clearly a popular destination for visitors, including children who can select a meal from their own menu. Pythius was treated with great respect and allowed to choose any table he wished, though no one thought to ask if he wanted a bowl of water. No doubt they assumed he would help himself from the brook, which ripples past the rear of hotel, when we had finished our meal.

The bar has a rustic feel, and offers a good range of real ales and a menu that contains something for everyone at quite reasonable prices. Yes – there is a restaurant too with an up-market menu – but naturally that is out of bounds for dogs.

The Walk

We had left our map behind, but that didn't matter, we enjoyed a gentle amble and a circular walk which took just under an hour without recourse to maps, as the footpaths are so well marked.

We watched a small family of ducks swimming in the brook at the back of the hotel, then turned right, took the small wooden bridge that links with the village cricket grounds, and found ourselves in a well groomed grassy area. Initially we had decided this would be enough as dark clouds were amassing – just a few runs round the ground would

wear Pythius out, then we could go on and explore the church.

It didn't quite work out like that. Pythius noticed a small gap in the greenery to the right close to the brook, and boldly walked through, ignoring the ball game we had planned. This entrance led to a tree-lined green path, which in turn led to a stile and a waymarker that directed us through a field of barley.

At the end of this path, we discovered a wooden gate tied shut with string and yet another green path,

Pythius says

Helen speaks of the hotel being child friendly, what she failed to say was that apart from a couple of delightful young children who appeared to be enjoying their meal, most of the visitors in the bar appeared to be a little older. Her age actually.

(Funny how she never mentions these things, which may be due to the fact she still seems to think she is a teenager – you will notice that her bus pass and all that goes with it is never mentioned either.)

Actually, that said, I found The Crown of Crucis a very friendly place. I liked the buzz, I liked the staff and must admit that the food smelt and looked delicious. The portions are certainly very generous.

As to the walk – well that turned out very well, thanks to my remarkable nose for footpaths. If it had been up to Helen and Auntie Liz I would have remained on the Cricket Grounds and spent the rest of the time admiring the resident ducks. Then I would have missed a rather enjoyable moment or two splashing about in the brook, which I encountered on the return journey, at the junction which led to the small tarmac road which we took to turn it into a circular walk. The water was clear and crisp, in fact everything a Border collie like me could ask for. I'd have stayed longer if it hadn't started to rain.

The only thing that almost caused me a bit of a problem was the very last stile which had wire netting fixed all round it, making it impossible for me slip through as I usually do. I had to jump up onto a very thin plank and then up and over – but eventually (with just a little help from the girls) I managed it.

I won't mention the drive home, the black clouds started to explode with rain which fell so thick and fast that the windscreen wipers didn't seem to work fast enough. I think Helen got quite scarred as the Mini swayed back and forward when big puddles disturbed by passing lorries flooded over us. But we did get home safely, despite the unexpected deluge. Helen said she had been driving on a wing and a prayer, but have no idea what that meant!

which eventually led to a small tarmac road. We came across this quite unexpectedly, so caution is advised at this point as cars do travel this road from time to time. A hand carved stone waymarker stands either side of this road, which urged us on, into another barley field, which eventually led to another green lane that curves back towards the village.

At one point we encountered the most fascinating wrought iron garden gate which was decorated with the most curious assortment of items, including a bicycle frame, a milk churn and several metal tools, which certainly warranted a second look. At the end of this lane it soon become apparent that you are going to hit the B4425. Fortunately this junction offers a choice and a smaller road to the right, leads back to the village, providing you take the first turn to the right on turning the first corner by the brook.

This little road turned out to be the one we had crossed previously on walking away from the village. On discovering the point where the two stone markers stood, we were able to turn left and return to the cricket ground and the car. Having encountered no livestock during this walk, and because well-placed waymarkers provide instructions at almost every turn, it almost impossible to get lost, so we rated it highly.

History

It's well known that the Romans were at Ampney Crucis. The village is but a few miles from the Chedworth Roman Villa that stands 3 miles north west of Fossebridge on the Cirencester–Northleach Road (A429). Unfortunately dogs are not allowed to walk round the ruins, which are open to the public from March to November.

We chose Ampney Crucis as it is a lesser-known Cotswold village, which gets its name from Ampney Brook that runs through the village, and its church Holy Cross. It's thought that the brook, which is a tributary of the Thames, takes its name from the Latin Amnis. Although the village has had several names, the name we use today appears to have been in use since 1535, though there are maps of the area dating back to 1632, which show its name as Holiroodeamney.

Ampney Crucis Church of the Holy Rood has the rare dedication of the Holy Cross and is referred to in the Doomsday Book (1086) as the Church of the Omenie Holy Rood – rood being the Saxon for cross.

Ardington
The Boar's Head

A rdington is one of those attractive downland villages that is so beautiful, one would assume it would be swarming with tourists during the summer season. Not so. Despite being only a few miles from the Ridgeway, it keeps itself to itself.

This is serious horse breeding country, so whilst you may occasionally encounter well groomed horses and their riders trotting down the green lanes, you will never find hordes of holiday-makers making the place their own. I find this one of its charms.

You will seldom see litter in the streets either and Ardington's hedges and gardens and are so well manicured, you may wonder if you have wandered onto a film set.

The Boar's Head stands in Church Street, which is to the left of the village if you enter via the small road linking Ardington to the A417 that runs through Wantage. Look for the church and you will find the pub.

And what a glorious little pub it is. It's one of those English hostelries that's been serving villagers and visitors for more than 150 years. I love its rustic look and the series of small rooms that lead to the main

restaurant at the rear. The eclectic mix of scrubbed tables and chairs, the glorious fresh flower arrangements that decorate the bar, and the general warmth of the place, make you feel welcome immediately.

On approaching, you will discover a sign on the main door saying Remove muddy boots, which suggests that walkers make this their watering hole. CAMRA members make for this pub too as it serves some superb local brews, including beers brewed on the nearby Lockinge Estate.

Those who remember Best Mate, the racehorse who was three times winner of the Cheltenham Gold Cup and considered one of the best loved horses in the history of horse racing in the UK, will smile when they discover that this local brewery is named Best Mates. The founders of the brewery – Darren Weal and Guy Bosley – will insist the name signifies they are best mates. However the licensee will give a wry smile and remind you that this is racehorse country and Best Mate was a horse no one will ever forget.

The food served here is superb, as local ingredients are used whenever possible and everything is cooked to order. Fish, which is delivered daily from Cornwall, features large on the menu too.

Obviously the quality of service and food is reflected in the price. This pub is not cheap. That said you get what you pay for – quality food served so perfectly it has your mouth watering the moment it is placed in front of you. It's the sort of place that Auntie Liz and I visit when we feel like a real treat. Light bites are served too and bowls of water are strategically placed in the bar area for visiting canines.

The Walk

The Ardington and Lockinge area is riddled with cycle routes and footpaths, so

Pythius says

This pub has got class – the staff treated me with great respect and even pointed out the large bowl of water that was placed in the first of several rooms for four-legged visitors in need of refreshment. They also went to great trouble to describe some of the walks we could take. They assured me I'd be in for a great time once lunch was over. It seems that whichever way you turn, there is a footpath or a right of way to enjoy, though I did hear Helen and Auntie Liz remark that they weren't all marked up very clearly. Apparently they found it difficult to tell if they were on private land when they reached the area surrounding Lockinge Church.

It's always tedious to begin a walk only to discover that Auntie Liz and Helen want to visit a church before I can be let off the lead. Things went from bad to worse when, on discovering a pond as the walk finally got under way, I found it was so securely fenced off I couldn't get in for a paddle. I did find water though, just before we reached the little road running through the next village, and was able to splash about to my heart's content. There was water by Lockinge Church too, but as a couple of swans were patrolling this little

brook that led to a series of small lakes close to the church grounds, I had to walk on without getting wet. Dogs like me know we should never try and share water with a couple of swans.

Must admit I found the big bronze horse rather formidable too, but once I realised it was a statue, I stopped panicking. All in all, quite a nice gentle walk with no real hazards except the swans.

the walk we took is but one of many in this unspoiled area. Unfortunately waymarkers are not always there when you want them, but most of the paths are so well worn and used, it's difficult to get lost.

Having asked permission from the licensee to leave my Mini in the pub car park, we started our walk from the Boar's Head.

To Pythius's annoyance we began by visiting Ardington's Holy Trinity Church, which stands next to the pub, as it is steeped with history, dating as it does from the early 13th century, with additions and embellishments made in 14th and 15th centuries. It's small but lavishly furnished and appears to be well cared for. Certainly worth a visit, once you have worked out just how to open the main door.

We then turned left, crossed the road and entered the first open gate on the right hand side, which appears to be leading into a green lane. It's not long before this opens up into a larger green and very well groomed space, flanked with trees on the right and a small fenced-off lake on the left, open only to those with a fishing permit. Naturally this annoyed Pythius who did all he could to gain access, but was defeated by the wire fence.

We then ambled through more and more green space, with a large cornfield on our left. The grass was lush and green and the abundance of trees on the right added an extra dimension to this walk. The trees attract birds and birds mean bird song.

We followed the path, which eventually leads to a small bridge passing over the brook, where Pythius was able to play for a while. The path then twists to the right. At this point you are approaching a small road lined with the attractive red brick Victorian houses of Lockinge, so it is necessary to put the dog on the lead.

Turn left when you reach the road, taking a moment to enjoy the scenic delights of this well laid out village with its line of neatly trimmed trees, then walk on to Lockinge Church. On the way, you will encounter a life-size bronze statue of a magnificent horse dominating a small green on the right.

This road narrows and eventually leads to All Saints Church, which stands in the grounds of Lockinge House. There is a stile that takes you into the church grounds, but unfortunately the doors are firmly locked against visitors.

At this point, having enjoyed the views, we turned and ambled home the way we had come. The whole walk took less than an hour and proved very pleasant.

History

Ardington with its near neighbour Lockinge form part of a large self-contained country estate established in the 19th century by Robert Loyd-Lindsay (later to become Baron Wantage) who rebuilt both Ardington and Lockinge, turning them into the model villages you see today.

Cassington
The Chequers

Because we had enjoyed ourselves so much during our visit to the Seven Tuns, Chedworth (see p33) Auntie Liz and I were delighted to discover that the licensee keeping that delightful pub had taken over one of our local pubs – the Chequers at Cassington.

Cassington is a small village that is reached off the A40 between the Wolvercote and Eynsham roundabouts, and is found by taking a turn at the only traffic lights on this stretch of the A40. It is a small village situated on gravel strata, which was recorded in the Domesday Book, though evidence of an earlier Bronze Age settlement in the area was discovered when excavating for gravel in the 1940s.

The Chequers was once a very small, homely kind of pub, but several years ago it was rebuilt and given a far more modern interior. Cotswold stone is still in evidence however, and a huge fireplace in the main bar area adds a touch of warmth on a chilly day.

There is a reasonably large car park at the rear, which you enter by taking the passage through an archway on the right hand side.

Pythius certainly enjoyed his visit to the Chequers as he was greeted by a group of friendly business men the moment he entered who seemed to understand that he was prepared to rise to their welcome. In fact they made such a fuss of him, we had trouble getting him to put his paws under the table.

I'd better say right from the start that this pub is not a cheap option, but you get what you pay for. The menu is bang up to date, with loads

of fascinating meals listed. Freshly cut sandwiches are available too, their fillings dependant on what the chef has in the kitchen when you order, which means it might be rare topside one day and home cooked

Pythius Says

Well the girls seemed to love the pub and from the way they tucked into their fish and chips, they enjoyed their beer too. They did get rather cross with me when I spent more time than I should talking to the locals, and kept instructing me to get under the table. I did in the end, but not before staying where I was for a moment to enjoy the fuss a rather nice gentleman was giving me.

If I am really honest I have to admit that the walk was not one of the best. Well it was OK, but there were no streams or rivers and the path was muddy and uninspiring. I don't think Helen and Auntie Liz enjoyed it that much either, they kept shaking their heads every time they came to a stile covered with signs. There are other footpaths in Cassington, but the one leading to the point where the River Thames meets the River Evenlode would have meant crossing the A40, not something even I would want to do. We could have kept on the footpath through the Worton buildings too, which would have finally come out at the Woodstock Road, but rain clouds were amassing, so we all made for home.

One thing I ought to warn you about are the many horses' hoof marks down the lane, which suggested that at any time at all we could have come head to head with a horse or two. Perhaps more? I don't think Helen noticed their marks in the mud as she was too busy being grumpy about the signs.

honey baked ham the next. We ordered beer battered cod and home made chips, which I can honestly say tasted so delicious, I'd rate our lunch amongst the best I have ever had. Other dishes listed included ragout of seafood and crab, roast guinea fowl and wild mushrooms, and confit of thyme pork belly.

As it is a Young's pub, we were able to enjoy a glass of Young's bitter, and Wells Bombardier was also on tap.

We left feeling happy to have such a well-run pub on our doorstep.

The Walk

Much to Pythius's annoyance we decided to visit the parish church first, as it stands but a stone's throw from the pub and we had to pass it anyway. St Peter's dates from the early 12th century. Traces of 14th century wall paintings and a fragment of an 18th century painting of the Last Judgment can be found here and the pews are thought to date back to the 15th century.

On leaving the church, exit the churchyard by the gate opposite the main door, which leads to a path alongside the village school. Turn right when you have passed the school and take the narrow passageway that will lead you to Bell Lane. You will then notice a foot-path marker to your right, but ignore that and turn left, the footpath sign pointing to Warton is just a few yards down the lane on the right hand side. You can't miss it – just look out for a rather strange stile created from iron and stone and covered with DO NOT notices. At first we assumed that the person who had erected these signs didn't like dogs very much, but on reading one of the signs we decided they had a sense of humour as one read: THE LANE IS PUBLIC, THE LAND IS PRIVATE. NOTE TO ALL DOGS – KEEP OWNERS ON A LEAD AND UNDER CONTROL.

Dare I suggest Pythius grinned when we read that out to him? Perhaps not – but we certainly did.

The stile leads to an open field, with a well worn path through the grass leading to another stile once you have passed a couple of trees that both have signs nailed to them asking walkers to clean up after their dogs. The next stile gave us more of the same, also an extra sign in blue asking walkers to keep to the path. There was a yellow waymarker erected by Oxfordshire County Council on the final stile, and only one sign warning us to keep dogs under control, so we began to relax.

We now found ourselves following a very muddy lane, passing fields of horses on the left and a high embankment on the right hiding the gravel pits from view. Only a large yellow sign saying: DANGER

DEEP EXCAVATION, suggested we were passing what was obviously a danger-ously deep body of water. The lane wanders on, finally opening out into a field, filled with homemade horse jumps and a large pile of manure. Once past the field and the farm house,

we met a small tarmac road and a sign telling us we had reached Worton Park, home of several offices and Worton Organic Gardens, where freshly harvested organic fruit and vegetables are always available.

Having had our fair share of signs on this walk, we turned and went back the way we had come, completing the walk in under an hour. Only when we had almost finsihed the walk did we spot yet another notice attached to a rusting piece of farm equipment positioned next to a small copse and very muddy pond, which said: OUT OF BOUNDS TO ALL. By our reckoning that was just one sign too many!

History

The excavations carried out on a 200 hectare site between Cassington and Yarton between 1989 and 1998 revealed evidence of continuous human habitation since Neolithic times (4000 – 1800 BC).

Chedworth
The Seven Tuns

On checking the Seven Tuns pub, Chedworth on the internet I found a website describing it as the 'Happiest pub in the Cotswolds' – and it was.

Having phoned to check that Pythius would be welcome, we marched into this unspoiled 17th century pub with confidence, and were greeted by an Australian barman with the warmest smile I have ever confronted. We were not just welcome, we were made *very* welcome.

Chedworth is one of those Cotswold gems that few people manage to find, because it is not on the main road. The village is just seven miles from Cirencester and five miles from Northleach, but it is tucked away off the beaten track, hugging the steep sides of a two mile long valley in which the a bubbling little tributary of the River Coln flows. The fact that Chedworth is 600 feet above sea level adds an extra charm to this glorious little village, with its undulating landscape which is not just picturesque, it is mind-blowingly beautiful. The creamy Cotswold stone houses circling the valley blend so perfectly with the trees and foliage that surrounds them, it is as if they emerged from the earth together, never to be separated.

As we drove down the hill towards the Seven Tuns, Auntie Liz and I were silent – there were no words to describe this find. We just knew we had discovered a pub and a village that was taking our breath away.

The date 1610 is written boldly over the main door and the pub-sign outside shows seven beer barrels, but the barman insisted that the name dates back to the time when the pub boasted seven chimneys rather than barrels of beer. Either way – it's a great atmospheric pub which has a timeless feel.

The thick wooden front door, which must date back several centuries, is difficult to open, but it makes a glorious clunk when you finally manage to get through and close it again. The main wood-lined bar is small, only three tables – but if you enter through another front door you will discover an equally historic restaurant and another room at the back. There's an attractive beer garden too.

Dogs are welcome in the bar. In fact the 'happy' barman was surprised I had even asked if Pythius could come in. Situated as it is in the middle of a popular walking area, this pub takes it for granted that many customers will arrive with their canine friends. Stepping into this bar, with its wooden trim and old settles, and old fashioned hospitality really is like stepping back in time.

The lunch menu is basic but who cares, the food is freshly cooked, well garnished and served promptly. The choice of real ales is impressive. It is a Young's pub, so were able to enjoy a glass of Wells Bombardier, which is synonymous with St George's Day and all things English, and enjoy its juicy malt and tangy hop flavours.

Pythius wasn't offered water as there is a large doggie bowl of cool water sitting opposite the pub, close to the bubbling little waterfall in the wall that signals the beginning of the Coln tributary which, having declared itself, runs underground, coming up again in the valley we walked after lunch.

Pythius Says

I love it when Auntie Liz and Helen are really happy, and they were certainly happy the day we visited Chedworth. I think their mood was partly due to the atmosphere pervading the pub – it was infectious.

We sat at a little table by the door, which enabled me to watch people coming in to order a drink and observe their reaction to the surroundings as they came in. It was all very positive. Everyone loved it. I certainly did as I was made as welcome as everyone else.

And the walk – well what can I say? It was absolutely fantastic as it contained simply everything a dog could wish for, including a delightful little brook that ran through the middle of the valley in which we walked.

It wasn't a big brook, in parts there was only a dribble of water coming through, but it tasted so sweet I kept going back for more. We passed through a small wood too, and loads of grassy fields filled to overflowing with dock leaves. As there were no cows around, the girls were relaxed and I was able to have a really great time. I was so exhausted when we returned to the car that I slept all the way home.

The Walk

We began exploring the area by taking the steep footpath opposite the pub, which leads to the church of St Andrew. The oldest parts of the present building – three lower stages of the tower, the nave arcade and the font – are Norman and date back to 1100. Like so many Cotswold churches its principal features are the fine 15th century Perpendicular windows, built when the prosperity of the Cotswold wool trade was at its height.

It's certainly a very impressive building, which serves an area that is geographically divided into Upper, Middle and Lower Chedworth, reflecting the position of each settlement on the stream that flows through the valley.

On returning to the road that runs past the pub, we took the footpath to the right of the pub which points the walker through a wooden gate that stands next to The Parsonage. This leads to a well-worn path that winds towards a small wooded area and then down to the valley. The number of waymarkers along the route is impressive, particularly as they point out numerous alternative routes and the many grassy lanes that criss-cross the area.

Should you wish you can follow the path through the valley and on to Fosse Bridge, following the little stream all the way round until you eventually come to Chedworth Roman villa. This is a three mile walk but well worth taking if you want to view the remains of the largest and most impressive Roman villas in the country. (The Roman villa can also be reached by taking the footpath past the Church – this is a far shorter walk – probably no more than a mile.)

We stayed in the valley, crossing many dog-friendly stiles as we walked the one and a half miles to Fosse Bridge before turning and gently ambling back. Because the paths are well walked and signed, there is no question of getting lost and the climb down to the valley and back not too arduous if you take it slowly.

This walk is exceptional and highly recommended if you are looking for lush scenic views and freedom to let the dog off the lead, providing he is kept under control.

History

When the Chedworth Roman Villa was discovered in 1864, excavators uncovered well preserved mosaics and 32 rooms, an under floor heating system, and Roman baths too. The villa is now owned and managed by the National Trust and has a well stocked visitors centre. It's certainly worth visiting if you are prepared to take the circular walk, which eventually leads you back to the church.

Obviously dogs are not permitted to walk round the ruins.

Cropredy
The Red Lion

Cropredy is now famous for its annual music festival; however, this delightful little village, situated near Banbury, made its real mark on the history of Oxfordshire in 1644 when King Charles I and his army travelled north from Oxford during the Civil War. When his army reached Cropredy Bridge, which crosses the River Cherwell, it was intercepted by the Parliamentary troops under Sir William Waller, and a bloody battle ensued. While the Royalists suffered few casualties, Waller lost more than 700 men, many deserting immediately after the battle. As the Royalists were low in food and supplies, they slipped away under cover of night, taking Waller's guns with them.

Fairport Convention began their link with the village when they were invited to play at the village fete in 1976. More than 700 people attended that event and so the Cropredy Music Festival was born. This festival is now a three-day event attracting more than 20,000 folk and rock music fans who flock to the village during August.

We weren't there for the festival – our intention was to walk a section of the Oxford canal path, which runs for 77 miles from Oxford to Coventry. Cropredy is the half-way point, which means that had we been energetic, we could have walked more than 35 miles in either direction – we didn't!

Friends who know the area well assured us that the Red Lion pub,

close to the canal was really dog-friendly, and that the canal would provide us with a fascinating walk – so we anticipated a great day.

As my beloved old Mini has been showing signs of age lately, Uncle John offered to drive us there in his smart car that never seems to break down. Besides I hate driving on motorways and you have to travel the M40 to get there. Cropredy is just a few miles from junction 11 north-bound along A361.

The Red Lion is easy to find once you get to the village as it stands next to the church in Red Lion Lane, a stone's throw from the canal.

This friendly little thatched pub, which dates back to 15th century, offers an extensive menu of snacks, grills and typical pub dishes. We

Pythius says

That pesky cat in the pub was really pushing his luck. I had my paws well under the table, yet the arrogant creature walked backwards and forwards, backwards and forwards, getting as close to our table as it dared. Actually, I rather like cats, but when they show off (and this one was certainly showing off), I do feel my hackles rising. But as Helen and Uncle John would have got really cross if I did anything that would spoil the day, I just closed my eyes and pretended to be asleep while they ate their lunch. The cat soon got bored with trying to wind me up and went off in a huff.

The walk was OK mostly – though I was rather disappointed to find that although we were in easy reach of water at all times, I wasn't able to jump in. It was far too deep and the banks were not dog-friendly. However, after trotting along the towpath for a while I began to get into the rhythm of things. Besides there was so much to see along the way and so many travelling dogs to greet. I rather envied them actually, and left wondering what I had to do to talk Helen into taking me on a boating holiday.

As for the famous battle scene, well we didn't see that until after lunch, it was what Helen called an add-on. Just a little extra which she thought I would enjoy. One day I will have to admit I am not really that fond of battle scenes. Yes, I can sense the fact they happened, that's what dogs can do, we feel the vibes through our paws, but it doesn't mean that such events excite us.

opted for soup and sandwiches, and a glass of Old Hooky beer, and were well satisfied. It was obvious many of the customers eating there were enjoying a trip on the canal, as the bar had a holiday feel, everyone seemed to be relaxed and happy. Speaking to some of the visitors while eating our lunch was great fun and got us into the mood for what was to prove a very jolly little walk.

We did notice a rather large black cat parading round the various rooms in this pub, which might have been a problem if Pythius disliked cats. Fortunately, he usually ignores them, so once he'd settled himself under the table he simply watched this arrogant feline walking among the tables for a while, then laid his head on the carpet and went to sleep.

The Walk

We left the pub and turned left towards the canal bridge, turning left again once we'd walked over the bridge, then down a series of steps onto the towpath. Turning right we then began our walk along the canal path. This is one of those walks where it is impossible to get lost, because all you do is keep to the canal path until you are ready to turn back. Yes, there are footpaths you can take along the way which will send you through fields and woods, but we chose to amble down the canal path covering the distance between bridge number 152 and bridge number 145, which was about one and a half miles, then went back the way we had come.

The great thing about this walk is that nearly everyone travelling the canal seemed to be in holiday mood. Waving at the travellers as they waved at us seemed to be the order of the day, and those we bumped into along the towpath were equally friendly. Once Pythius accepted that he wouldn't be able to get into the canal for a splash-about in the water, he seemed to embrace the friendly nature of this walk. He certainly enjoyed greeting the many canal dogs he met along the way – some walking the

towpath, but most travelling on the attractive canal boats that waited patiently to enter the many locks we encountered. By the time we had finished the walk, Uncle John and I felt we had been on holiday too!

Later, before returning home, we walked down to Cropredy Bridge to see the site of the Civil War battle, which is about five minutes walk from the canal bridge where we first started.

History

Besides its music festival and famous battle, Cropredy is also known for its curfew bell, which is rung at 8 p.m. on Tuesdays and Fridays. This tradition was set up by Roger Lupton, who lost his way when returning from nearby Chacombe in a fog in 1512. Only the sound of the Cropredy bell tolling in the distance helped him to reach home safely. In gratitude he set up a fund to pay for the clock to be wound and the bell to be rung several times a day – beginning at 4am. Although this tradition continues, today's bell ringers have modified the schedule, and only ring the curfew bell twice a week.

Cumnor
The Bear and Ragged Staff

Pythius and I had no companion with us when we called into the Bear and Ragged Staff, Cumnor – all our friends were busy, so we soldiered on without them.

The Bear and Ragged Staff is an imposing building that stands on the Appleton road, just past the village duck pond.

Surprisingly it has only operated as a pub since the middle of the 19th century. It's said to have taken its name from an older hostelry nearby known as the Black Bear, which is thought to have been destroyed by fire a few years earlier.

As the Bear and Ragged Staff is close to my home, it is a pub I have used frequently over the years. Indeed, I remember it from years back when the waiting staff wore traditional black and white uniforms when serving in what was then an exclusive restaurant at the rear.

That restaurant has been redesigned now, but the old bar I have always loved so much, with its worn polished flagstones and roaring log fire, remains untouched.

The pub went through a difficult patch a few years ago, but it is now being run by an enthusiastic entrepreneur who is doing everything he can to promote real ale and local produce. The large restaurant extension, built during a refurbishment a few years ago, is now proving a popular place to meet for lunch.

Because the new owner wishes to promote the game season during the autumn and winter months, he holds special game dinners to celebrate the woodlands and farmland which surround this lovely place. Unfortunately dogs are not allowed to attend those dinners; however

Pythius is always welcome in the bar area, and enjoys the fuss the staff make of him when he calls in before or after a walk. He was even offered a dog biscuit during his last visit, which really perked him up no end as he is a dog who enjoys attention, and an extra biscuit never goes amiss. Water is always readily available should he need it.

The Walk

I must admit that the walk we take to Bessels Leigh is not the most exciting one we have ever done. The landscape is flat, and there is no river for dogs to splash about in, unless the ditch on your left, created to carry water from Cumnor village pond to the Ock and the Thames, is doing its job. This ditch is named the Osse ditch, from the old English wase, meaning mud, so as its name suggests, it is not often full of water. Actually, during high summer, the ditch is often hard to spot as vegetation hides it from view.

However a walk is a walk, and if you are prepared to use your eyes, there is always something interesting or unusual to see. The silence that surrounds the area is a big bonus, and something you can really appreciate if walking alone with just a dog for company. Only the plod, plod of Pythius's paws moving in a forward direction disturbs the peace.

With our back to the Bear and Ragged Staff, we always turn right and after a few yards join a footpath sign-posted Bessels Leigh. You will notice the cricket pavilion on the left almost as soon as you take the path.

Now follow the track, ignoring a footpath sign about 100 yards away on the right as this leads back to the road through Cumnor; besides

---

Pythius says

Well, as Helen says, this was not the most exciting walk, as there was no river and not many places where I could run round and round and have fun as I like to do. But it was a nice autumn day, the people in the pub had been kind to me and I must admit there are times when I rather enjoy having Helen all to myself. She chats on to me about this, that and the other as we walk, and I keep giving her those meaningful looks that suggest I am listening, when really I am keeping my eyes open for something to play with. It's all very companionable. Who cares what the countryside looks like if you are in good company?

which, you will see a sign asking you to keep your dog on a lead if you take that track.

The lane we take finally peters out, but don't worry: it opens out into a large field. You will notice the footprints of countless walkers defining a path that runs alongside the field, with the hedgerow and ditch on your right. Keep walking for about a mile until you reach a wooded area. A way sign will mark the way.

Having reached the trees on the far side of the field, turn left, then make for an opening in the corner, which is sometimes difficult to find during high summer, when it is partially covered with vegetation. Walk straight through the small wood, keeping a fence on your right hand side.

Carry on, straight through a galvanised gate, until you come to a small footbridge that leads to another galvanised gate. Now swing left and cross the field towards the road; like all the paths on this walk, it is easy to identify as people walk this way often. If you keep walking in line with the telephone wires, a waymark in the corner of the field will lead you to the road and Bessels Leigh.

There is a great pub at Bessels Leigh, but unfortunately they don't allow dogs inside, so at this point you can either return the way you have come or turn it into a longer walk by heading for the Eight Bells, Eaton where dogs are welcome (see page 51). Unfortunately that would mean walking on tarmac. However, as it is not a busy road, you can probably let your dog off the lead, providing you take care and listen out for approaching vehicles.

We turned back, having walked about a mile, enjoying the fact that the scenery always looks different when walking the other way.

If you are feeling more energetic, you could carry on for another mile to the village of Appleton. Yes, there's a nice pub there too, but they don't welcome dogs either.

History

The Bear and Ragged Staff has a rich history, for although it is now a popular public house and restaurant, it was used as an army billet during the Civil War, when Richard Cromwell, son of Oliver Cromwell, is said to have lived there. It is thought that the hole chiselled out of the lintel above the fireplace in the main bar marks the spot where Richard Cromwell moved a royal crest.

Deddington
The Unicorn Inn

Visitors to Deddington, which stands on the A4260 16 miles north of Oxford and 6 miles south of Banbury, can be forgiven for assuming that this historic village is a town. Not so. Although its market square is dominated by a Town Hall and its football team is called Deddington Town Football Club, Deddington is definitely a village.

Deddington is also unusual in that it was once dominated by a castle, built to the east of the village, which was commissioned by Bishop Odo of Bayeaux (the half-brother of King William I) soon after the Norman Conquest.

Unfortunately only the castle grounds exist now. The eight acres on which the castle once stood are now a picturesque recreational area where people can walk amongst grassy banks surrounded by trees, and admire the many wild flowers that flourish on this unspoiled spot. This is where we walked after lunch at the 17th-century Unicorn Inn, an imposing whitewashed building in the market square.

There was absolutely no problem about bringing Pythius into this

pub. When a member of staff noticed us hesitating at the front door, unsure if we could go in or not, we were greeted with warmth and told dogs were always welcome in the snug on the left hand side. So in we went – all three of us, Pythius, me and Auntie Liz. Pythius was immediately offered a bowl of water, which as usual arrived before our beer was served. He was then patted on the head and told he was a good boy. Only when he appeared to have settled were we offered the bar menu and asked if we would like a drink.

Pythius says

Well, I must admit that walking round this village while Helen and Auntie Liz admired its many little shops didn't thrill me that much. I certainly got really fed up when they took it in turns to rummage around the Deddington Antique Centre in the Market Square that they described as an Aladdin's cave – whatever that means. When they then spent almost as much time admiring the produce in Mr Eagles' food hall next door, I really did begin to get agitated. Had they stayed there another five minutes I am sure I would have cocked a leg at the voluptuous life-sized model of a happy butcher that stood outside leering at me. But I didn't. They were having such a lovely time, how could I possibly spoil it for them. I knew my time would come if I was patient.

The castle grounds were great. Lots of space, loads of trees and glorious smells of hares, rabbits, badgers and deer. I think Mr Fox walks through occasionally too. I wish we had a recreational ground like this in my own village.

There's something delightfully old fashioned and homely about The Unicorn Inn, and that's not because of its age. The menu offers simple, no-nonsense reasonably priced dishes, the choice of real ales is impressive and the service is really friendly.

We enjoyed the 'olde world', country town atmosphere and the feeling that we were in a time warp that was projecting us back to that

period when country inns, pubs and hotels were run by families who were prepared to go out of their way to serve their guests.

The Walk

The village of Deddington sits on top of a ridge overlooking the Cherwell Valley and is surrounded by lush, picturesque countryside. The River Swere forms its northern boundary, whilst the River Cherwell, and a parallel stream known as South Brook, divides it from Duns Tew. There are, therefore many superb walks that take in the nearby villages of Clifton, Hempton and

Duns Tew. But, after exploring the town we were looking for somewhere that Pythius could run free and we could enjoy a gentle amble that would not be too exacting.

Staff at the Unicorn suggested we visit the castle grounds, just a five-minute walk away, as this space, which is managed by English Heritage, is where everyone takes their dogs.

So, after crossing the Market Square we took the Castle Road that leads to Clifton, turning right into a lane leading to the Castle Grounds after walking for just a few minutes.

Once we had reached the grounds, we were able to let Pythius run free as the grounds are enclosed by hedgerows, mature trees and banks that include remnants of the castle moat. It's certainly a very ancient and attractive space. There are seats strategically placed to enable visitors to rest and admire the view and lots of room for dogs to run and play. For those not looking for a long walk, it proves an ideal place.

History

This beautiful north Oxfordshire village with its charming ironstone buildings has a particular claim to fame – it is the only parish in England to be granted its own Coat of Arms, which can be can be seen

in a relief fixed on the wall of the Town Hall in the Market Square. The arms represent the three manors that make up the Parish – Castle of Windsor, Duchy and Christ Church. Its motto: preo on anan gebundene, written in Early English rather than Latin, means three joined together in one, and also refers to the three villages of the Parish – Deddington, Clifton and Hempton.

Dorchester-on-Thames
The Fleur de Lys

If you enjoy the sensation of being surrounded by 1,000 years of history that you can see as you walk, in the knowledge that you are also stepping on 2,000 years of history that you cannot see but can feel, then Dorchester-on-Thames is the place to visit.

This ancient place is three miles north west of Wallingford and eight miles south east of Oxford, just above the Thames' confluence with its tributary the River Thame.

Because the area dates back to the Iron Age and is bounded with water on three sides, it became an important place for both communications and defence during the Iron Age. This is probably why the Romans built the town of Dorocina here too and why the Saxons built the first cathedral in Wessex on the spot where the present abbey now stands. Actually, this lovely little villages rates as one of our oldest cities, although it's hard to imagine that now as it is so small, though visitors soon sense the rich slice of history that settles on its beautiful old buildings.

Auntie Liz and I usually take Pythius to the Fleur de Lys, a 16th-century inn that stands in the High Street and very close to the lane in

Pythius says

Helen is constantly telling me that the stretch of river running past Dorchester is where the famous writer Jerome K. Jerome, who wrote *Three Men in a Boat*, stopped for a while with his two companion as they made their way along the Thames from Kingston to Oxford. She says he described Dorchester as a delightfully peaceful old place. Well it is – but I think I should point out that the dog Montmorency, who was supposed to have accompanied them on this trip, was a figment of his imagination. He didn't exist! I am sure they would have had even more fun if they had taken a real dog like me on that river journey. But they didn't.

Helen and Auntie Liz certainly enjoy it when I share their walks and do the things that real dogs do, like rolling in cow-pats, jumping into rivers and herding them both through stiles and gates.

Had Montmorency been real, I wonder if he would have sensed the air of history that surrounds this area? I admit to gaining a great deal of enjoyment from running up and down the Dyke Hills that Helen mentioned, as dogs can sense the age of such mounds. Indeed, I often wonder if Iron Age man used dogs to help them defend their fortress. And if so what did Iron Age dogs look like? Such speculations are great fun.

which we always begin our walk. We are usually allowed to keep the car in the car park at the rear, while we take Pythius for a walk, but we never assume this is our right and always ask first.

It's a very cosy, friendly place that serves a good selection of real ales and well-cooked reasonably priced basic pub meals that are beautifully presented. The last meal I ate there looked like something that had jumped straight out of a glossy gourmet magazine. It tasted great too, even though it was a very simple dish. On a warm summer's day we usually eat in the pub's lovely garden where we can admire its old cob wall in the car park.

Pythius is always made welcome and offered water as soon as he has placed his paws under the table. As Dorchester is one of his favourite places, he rates the Fleur de Lys highly too.

The Walk

There are many walks you can enjoy in this area. Before beginning any walk around Dorchester it is certainly worth visiting the abbey, only a couple of minutes walk from the Fleur de Lys.

We always begin our walk by turning right out of the pub and heading down the High Street, past Bridge View Cottage and right just before you reach the bridge. This will lead you to Wittenham Lane, which is the public footpath to the Thames and Little Wittenham. As you head for an open field you may notice a small table standing besides one of the gardens which is laden with fresh vegetables and plants, with a notice inviting walkers to make their choice and place their money through the door of the bungalow with the privet hedge. We often buy bags of home grown tomatoes during the summer

months and munch them while we walk, as they are both ripe and delicious. You will now see the outline of Wittenham Clumps dominating
the skyline. (For further information on these historical mounds see
p89.) Follow the footpath along the edge of the field to a metal kissing
gate in the corner. If you keep the Dyke Hills (easily recognisable
double rampart of earthworks that once protected a late Iron Age settlement) on your right all you have to do to reach the Thames Path is
walk across the next field. Unfortunately, the last time we attempted
this walk there was a notice warning walkers there were cows with
their calves here and that they should keep well away from them. So
we turned back to the kissing gate, and keeping the Dyke Hills on our
left continued walking the footpath round the field, which eventually
led us back to Dorchester through the back streets. This was not the
walk we had intended, but it provided a fascinating glimpse of old
Dorchester and the houses behind the main street.

Had we ignored the cows we would have turned left on reaching the
Thames, going over a footbridge which crosses the River Thame at its
confluence with the Thames and just enjoyed the view, before turning left,
walking up other side of the river which leads back to Dorchester Bridge.

For a slightly longer walk we sometimes follow the Thames until we
reach Day's Lock, where the annual Pooh Sticks Festival takes place
in early spring, then cross the river and proceed to Wittenham Clumps.
Pythius adores it when we take that walk, which takes at least an hour
each way – sometimes longer.

History

The abbey we see today in Dorchester dates from the 12th century,
replacing two Saxon cathedrals. While other abbeys throughout the
land suffered during the Dissolution of the Monasteries during Henry
VIII's time, the abbey stood firm, thanks to a wealthy man who paid
the king £140, which was the value of the lead on the chancel roof. He
then bequeathed the abbey church to the parish of Dorchester in his
will.

The tower was rebuilt in 1602 and major repairs took place in the
mid-18th century. More repairs took place in the 20th century, with a
major refurbishment programme in 1998. The Abbey remains the spir-
itual heart of the village and is used regularly to stage concerts and
music festivals. It is certainly worth a visit.

Eaton
The Eight Bells

Some pubs seem to change hands frequently. The Eight Bells, Eaton near Appleton, south Oxfordshire, is one of them. Over the years it has had a steady stream of owners. However, it seems to have settled now and appears to be in very capable hands. Pythius and I certainly enjoyed our last visit, which we made in the company of Beverly, her miniature chocolate poodle named Rolo, and a mutual friend named Steve, who rather enjoys celebrating Fridays by going out for a meal.

You reach Eaton (not to be confused with Water Eaton near Kidlington) by taking a right hand turn if travelling from Oxford on the A420 towards Fyfield and Kingston Bagpuize. The first thing you notice on reaching this delightful little hamlet is the silence. It's so far from a main road, nothing can be heard but birdsong and the gentle pad, pad, pad of dogs' paws walking through the long grasses.

Many years ago this pub was known for its gnomes. Yes, gnomes! Garden gnomes. Hundreds of them decorated the grassy area in front of the pub. I remember how we used to try and count them, but after a couple of drinks we all came up with a different number. There are no gnomes now, just lots of locals enjoying the fact that their pub has been brought back to life again after being closed for 18 months.

The pub is small; it has one public bar and a lounge bar with a small restaurant adjoining it. The public bar is gorgeous, loads of dark wood and rustic old tables and chairs. Several real ales, including a couple from West Berkshire Brewery, are on tap. The other two rooms are best described as homely.

As we arrived the moment the landlord was opening up we were able to choose where we sat – how were we to know that we had bagged the table that the regulars normally make their own? They were too polite to ask us to move, but we were aware that we had done something wrong.

The food is typical pub grub, reasonably priced, nicely cooked, and served with a smile. We did have a problem when it came to paying the bill however. On brandishing my piece of plastic, I was greeted with the words: "We only take cash." A silence filled the room, I was suddenly conscious everyone assembled was waiting to see what I would do next.

Pythius says

Perhaps I shouldn't say this, particularly as Beverly is one of Helen's friends, but that Rolo dog of hers is a real pain. He's one of those posh dogs that is so posh you half expect to find his pedigree documents hanging round his neck so that everyone can pay due homage when he enters a room.

I think he believes he's human – which would account for the way he jumped straight up on the seat next to his mistress immediately we began getting ourselves settled. I gave a low growl to warn him this was not permitted and that he should put his paws under the table, but he just tossed his head in the air, as if he had a divine right to do whatever he wished, then looked the other way.

I don't think the kindly man who served us thought much of that either, but he was far too polite to say anything. Actually Rolo looked so full of himself as he sat there, I half expected his mistress to lay out a knife and fork for him, and tuck a napkin under his chin so he could eat at the table too. Gosh I was cross! Really cross! Dogs like this give us canines a bad name. What's the point of me trying to be an ambassador for dog-friendly pubs (which I am) if my companions let me down like that?

I tried to let him know that I'm a fully paid up member of CAMRA, and therefore a dog to be reckoned with. I thought that would put him in his place, but the silly creature had no idea what I was talking about, so we just agreed not to speak further.

There were moments when I was tempted to break the silence by teasing him about his name. After all, how can a dog that's named after a chocolate dare suggest he is posh?

Yes, the walk is just tarmac, tarmac and even more tarmac, until you get to a spot where the road reaches the riverbank. Not an inspiring walk in some ways, but in others it was fine as I was able to enjoy the scents left by the wild things that frequent the area when dusk falls.

Rolo was intent on catching a rabbit or two as we walked, but he didn't find any. Actually, I spotted a couple in one of the fields we passed. Had I felt more kindly disposed towards this snobbish little dog, perhaps I would have told him – but I didn't.

Thanks to Steve who managed to come up with a £20 note, we managed to scratch the required amount together, but we only just made it. Perhaps I should have asked before assuming I could use my credit card to pay the bill; it just hadn't occurred to me that cash-only pubs still existed these days.

The Walk

With your back to the pub, turn right onto the little tarmac road that winds through the hamlet past various farms and the occasional cottage, and just keep walking. Yes, that's all you have to do. This might sound rather dull, particularly as the walk does not take in any fields, or explore woods or copses, but actually it is all very peaceful. Very few cars travel along this road; in fact, we walked for an hour and only encountered two cars and they were travelling very slowly.

Now and again, if you turn left and peep through the hedgerow you will discover some lovely views of the river, which Pythius found very frustrating as he could see and smell water, but was not allowed to venture forth.

After about ¾ of a mile you will come to the Thames bank and the point where a ferry once took customers to the Ferryman Inn, Bablock Hythe, which stands on the opposite bank. Unfortunately the ferry does not operate now.

Should you wish to extend your walk you can follow the footpath sign, which takes you on along the towpath for 2½ miles, until you reach Northmoor. Or, if you fancy extending it to Cumnor, turn right at the bridleway signposted Cumnor, that you will also spot at this point, close to a wooden gate. This walk will take you past the Physic Well, which is partly hidden in the trees to the left. This is now a muddy spring but was once greatly valued as a source of healing waters. Moist ground and mud will identify the spot.

History

Eaton was originally sited lower down the hill towards Bablock Hythe and the River Thames, but it is thought to have moved to its present position after the Black Death which wiped out the entire hamlet during the 14th century.

Edge Hill
Castle Inn

Yes, I do realise that the map puts Edgehill firmly a mile inside the Warwickshire border, but its postal address is Banbury, Oxfordshire. As the Castle Inn rates as one of the most unusual pubs that Pythius and I have ever visited, how could I resist placing it in this book? The turning is off the A422 Stratford road 6 miles from Banbury.

Built on the summit of Edgehill, some 700 feet above sea level, this historic pub overlooks the battlefield of Edge Hill, where Englishman fought Englishman in the first major battle of the English Civil War. Its octagonal tower marks the very spot where King Charles I raised his standard and summoned his troops around him to prepare for war in 1642.

Building began on the tower in 1742 to commemorate the 100th anniversary of the battle and it was opened in 1759, the anniversary of

Cromwell's death. It became an inn in 1822. In 1922 the inn was acquired by the Hook Norton Brewery and has remained a Hook Norton pub ever since. This means that those superb real ales brewed by Hook Norton Brewery and keenly enjoyed by enthusiasts are readily available. There's also a special brew named Castle Ale (also brewed by Hook Norton Brewery) which really hits the spot when you have walked more than three miles over difficult terrain and are really ready for liquid refreshment.

The inn, which is built of local ironstone, comprises two bar areas, one of which is filled with replicas of armour and weapons used in the battle. The other, on the left of the main door, is a small dog-friendly public bar where the locals congregate.

As we had walked for almost two hours and had not come across a stream or river, Pythius was badly in need of a drink. On requesting water we were told the dog bowl stood outside by the back door, so Uncle John offered to take Pythius outside for a much needed drink, but recent winds had blown the bowl (well actually it was a blue plastic box) out of sight. The kindly landlord finally discovered it half way down the path, filled it with water and presented it to a very thirsty dog, while we sipped Castle Ale with as much enthusiasm as Pythius lapped up his water.

The menu is standard pub fare, but perfect for walkers who have built up an appetite and are happy to tuck into steaming bowls of home made soup served with crusty bread, or doorstep sandwiches served with salad and crisps.

The bar area is homely. There's nothing posh about this pub as it caters for walkers, who like us, come wearing muddy boots and are not concerned about décor.

The views from the pub's beer garden on a clear day are simply amazing as the foothills of the Welsh Mountains are visible and there are times when visitors can enjoy a glimpse of the Wrekin in Shropshire. The distant hills of Broadway and the Malverns can also be seen at times, so you don't have to be interested in history and ancient battles to enjoy this area. There is much to see and admire providing you have the stamina to cope with very hilly terrain.

The Walk

It's worth noting right from the start that although this walk is only about three and a half miles long, it does involve some steep climbs and slippery mud during wet weather. But if you enjoy a challenge and want to soak up the atmosphere of this historic place – then take a deep breath and go for it.

We parked in the Castle Inn's car park that stands opposite the inn, then began by walking a narrow stone-lined passage way that can be found next to the car park, between Cavalier Cottage and Rupert House. This enclosed lane leads to a stile and then a small road.

Turn left at this point and walk the road until you reach the village of Ratley. Pythius didn't enjoy this part of the walk very much as I put him on the lead even though very little traffic passes this way.

On reaching a junction, cross straight over the road and follow the way signs that mark the Centenary Way. This starts as a track, but soon opens out into a large field that swings to the left. Skirt the field, keeping a line of trees to your right until you come to a galvanised kissing gate and another waymarker. We were stumped when we arrived at this point as the marker appeared to point to a path right across a ploughed field. No footprints or tracks suggesting other walkers had passed this way. Deciding to take the easy option, as it was freshly ploughed and very muddy, we skirted the field, keeping the hedge to our right until we came to a little wooden footbridge on the far side that led to another large ploughed field. At this point we followed the marks of a tractor which cut straight across the field, leading to a gap in the hedge and another road.

Much to Pythius's disgust, we put him back on the lead and

Pythius says

What Helen hasn't told you is that I was having a really wonderful time jumping around in the mud in that first big ploughed field, but they decided to spoil my fun by walking round the edge of the second one. They really are spoilsports at times, and all because Uncle John has a really clean car and doesn't take kindly to it being covered with mud.

I must admit this is not an easy walk, even for a Border collie like me, as there are so many ups and downs. I certainly found those steep slippery steps difficult towards the end of the walk.

But the pub was warm and friendly, and once the landlord found a bowl of water for me, I just slept until they finished their lunch. Gosh I was thirsty – there wasn't a single stream to be found on this walk, so please remember this if you take your dog on this route on a hot day because dogs get just as thirsty as humans!

followed the marker sign pointing left past a line of bungalows.

Having passed Battle Lodge we soon came to a road junction, crossed over and discovered a delightful woodland path running along the top of the escarpment and parallel to the road.

Once you have walked through an attractive woodland (which doesn't take long) you come to a post covered with waymarkers. Turn right at this point and you will encounter a series of steps descending at an alarming rate. We noticed that a bunch of flowers were tied to this post, and on noticing just how steep and slippery these steps were, wondered if someone had died trying to climb or descend them. These steps are known as Jacob's Ladder, and for good reason – once you reach the bottom and look back to view the flight of steps you have taken, you will feel they really do appear to reach up to the heavens.

On reaching the bottom of the steps you will face a large field, which is marked by hundreds of footsteps that have crossed it to the wooden kissing gate at the bottom leading to a path which runs alongside a private house with a magnificent vegetable garden. A sign by the house invites walkers to come in and buy fresh vegetables.

It was at this point that Uncle John's sense of humour got the better of him, as he tried to persuade me to buy freshly dug potatoes and a bag of purple sprouting seen growing there. As we had just clambered down one of the steepest slopes I have encountered for some considerable time and had a steep climb ahead of us, I declined, though I don't think I'd have got fresher vegetables. Uncle John was testing my

love of freshly harvested food – did I really love it so much that I would be prepared to drag a bag full of produce uphill as we began our ascent to the Castle Hill? The answer was No, with a capital N. But I did gain face by suggesting that we could drive back to the house once we had finished our walk.

On reaching another road, we turned left and walked through the beautiful village of Radway, with its lovely little Methodist chapel and The Grange which turned out to be the most important building in the village. Its grounds were pretty impressive too. We did laugh on seeing one of those notices that local councils put up when a resident has requested an extension to their property, and seeks local permission for it to go ahead. It was an application for a helicopter pad in the grounds of The Grange.

"Gosh," remarked Uncle John, "What kind of country are we travelling through? In Witney these signs usually request permission to erect a garage." We looked round at the manicured lawns and hedges we were passing and laughed at the way life is.

Reaching the church we continued for a few moments, then followed the road that veered left past a pond and some thatched cottages on towards a lane and another kissing gate.

At this point it is uphill all the way, for in the far distance, if you look up, you can see the turret of the Castle Inn. This is where the battle took place. Just keep going, pausing to turn and enjoy the view if you want an excuse to stop for breath as this climb is quite steep. Don't worry though, the pub stays open all day, so a glass of real ale always awaits, regardless of the time you finally reach the top.

History

The battle of Edgehill only lasted three hours. While both sides were made up of more than 14,000 men, neither side was able to make headway and the fighting ceased when darkness fell. Although no one claimed a decisive victory Charles I is thought to have 'won', insofar as the road to London was now open to him. He failed to take advantage of this opportunity, however, and so missed his best chance to take London.

Enstone
The Crown

There's Church Enstone and Neat Enstone, but few who live in the area bother with these distinctions now. They just use the name Enstone when referring to this delightful cluster of houses that lies about four miles south-east of Chipping Norton on the A44.

This is where Auntie Kate and Polly the Labrador live, so Pythius and I visit Enstone often to enjoy a companionable lunch at The Crown, Mill Lane, which stands close to the parish church. Find the church and you will find the pub.

The Crown is a picturesque 17th century inn that oozes with atmosphere and serves some superb locally brewed cask ales.

Naturally this pub is dog-friendly, it couldn't be otherwise given the lush undulating, wooded countryside surrounding it. Kate chose to live here because of the unspoilt beauty of her surroundings, which she and Polly walk daily.

A dog bowl filled with cold water is placed beside the inglenook fireplace in the main bar area. Dogs who know this make for it immediately while their masters order their drinks.

One of the delightful things about The Crown is the number of locals it attracts. Some find a quite corner where they can relax with a daily paper, which they can pick up in the entrance, others use it because they enjoy lively meaningful conversation.

Kate uses it because the food is scrumptious and the service friendly. Besides, this is where most of her local friends congregate during the weekend. When we join her here during the winter, Polly and Pythius sit as close to the wood fire as they can when they first enter, but soon move away once they have warmed themselves up.

In the summer we all sit in the attractive little walled garden outside. Yes, there is a restaurant too, but dogs are not allowed in there.

The last time we called we enjoyed a home cooked Sunday lunch served with all the trimmings which proved as good as anything I would have prepared at home.

As all the food served here is cooked by the imaginative chef patron Tony Warburton, who has a flair for creating flavours that speak for themselves, it really is worth scanning the blackboard menu carefully

as it often contains hidden treasures you seldom find in country pubs. Filled baguettes are available too.

Hook Norton ales, with guest beers such as Timothy Taylor's Landlord, are on tap, as well as Cotswold Lager.

In other words a perfect country pub that combines well with a dog walk.

The Walk

There are two really good walks at Enstone. The first can be as long or as short as you want it to be. With your back to the pub, turn left towards the church and take the narrow lane beside the parish church, St Kenelm, which was built around 1180.

This lane leads to a gate and a green lane and eventually a stile that takes you into a large scrubby meadow where you will find rosebay willow herb, morning primrose and an abundance of clover during the summer months. It is a glorious unkempt meadow where the dog can run free without fear of bumping into livestock.

A well-walked path leads you through the field to a small stream at the bottom and another field, then another. In fact you can walk for a mile or more before reaching a wooded area and eventually Heythrop

Pythius says

I have done this walk often, once with Uncle John, and part of it with Auntie Liz, but mostly with Auntie Kate and Polly. Now that Polly and I have really got to know each other, I guess I love walking with them most, because Polly and I can get on with the walk while they chat.

I also enjoy being with Auntie Kate because she is not scared of cows, and can guide us safely through a field of bovine beasts without any panic. (Oh why can't Helen do that?)

If they advance towards us, Kate simply waves her map in the air and they immediately turn round and walk in another direction. Sometimes she just talks and smiles at them, which seems to work too. Gosh Auntie Kate is an amazing woman with a real knack for handling four legged creatures. She certainly isn't frightened when we meet up with them.

Whilst there is not much water on this walk, we pass through such beautiful undulating pastures, that it really does rate as one of those special walks that can be done again and again and again. Each season offers something different. I love it.

And the pub – well what can I say? It's perfect. I feel so comfortable there. So does Polly. We often head for the fire when we visit on a cold winter's day, but soon put our paws under the table because it is so hot.

Park. We tend to stay in the first field and let Pythius run free until he is exhausted.

The second walk, which is our favourite, but is at least three miles long, will take you past the ancient Hoar Stone Burial Chamber that dates back to the Neolithic period, though it could be even earlier.

To view the stone and enjoy the second walk, you must find your way to the A44 and the centre of Enstone by taking the road directly opposite the pub, having crossed the road. You will spot a waymarker pointing the way.

Having passed several houses, and admired the dog-shaped weather vane on the last building as the lane veers left, keep going, you will soon find yourself in a narrow lane, with further waymarkers urging you to go on. You may also notice a rough hand painted sign asking you to keep dogs on the lead.

This lane finally meets a field. But first you have to cross a wooden stile that is not as safe as it should be. Rotten wood causes it to wobble slightly. So take care.

At this point it is tempting to assume you must walk straight across the field to a stile straight ahead. Don't. Keep to the right, for as you do so you will see another stile, which leads to a series of fields and a little stream. Keep going through two more fields and you will find yourself in a lane that takes you to the centre of Enstone and the main road.

Turn left along the lane, then left on reaching the main road, past the well stocked village shop and Post Office until you spot Cox's Lane on the right.

Cross the main road with care and follow Cox's Lane for about a quarter of a mile until you pass the village sports ground and meet up with the B4022.

Once again cross with great care and take the small road opposite which passes the Hoar Stone Burial Chamber towards the hamlet of Fulwell.

The Hoar Stone is just a few yards down this road, but is so heavily shrouded with dense foliage, you could easily pass it unnoticed as you walk by. It stands on your right hand side at the edge of a small wood. Although you will be tempted to photograph this ancient stone, take time to compose the picture or (like me) you will be disappointed to find all you get is a brown blob, due to the depth of dark shadows that fall on this ancient site.

You will not have to walk far to reach the hamlet of Fulwell, which comprises just a few cottages, one of which bears a blue plaque commemorating the life of the farm labourer and shepherd Mont

Abbott, whose life was written up by Sheila Stewart in her lyrical book *Lifting the Latch*, a social history that spans almost all of the 20th century.

To Pythius's annoyance this is the point where Kate and I spend a few moments absorbing the atmosphere of this delightful hamlet and reflecting on the history that this gentle shepherd wove into the area. (Polly didn't seem to mind, she has done this walk many times, and knows her mistress admires the blue plaque and all it stands for).

Now take the footpath on the left hand side which takes you through a gate and a large field. A small, but docile herd of cows are often grazing here, but they have never caused us any trouble. Just keep to the field edge, following the path to gate and another stile.

There will come a time when the path divides and offers a choice. Take the right hand path which leads to the A44. Because traffic speeds down this road at a tremendous rate, please take great care before crossing as this really is a dangerous road.

Once safely across, all is well and you can enjoy walking through an atmospheric wooded area in which your dog can run free. It finally opens out to a field that leads to a number of cottages and a narrow lane that eventually opens out to another tarmac road. You have now reached the hamlet of Cleveley. Bear left, then take the right hand track past a large pond (some might call it a lake) and an attractive house. Bypassing the house and keeping to the path that bears left, you can now enjoy walking down a lovely little country lane, which will eventually take you back to the B4022. Cross the road and take the lane straight ahead, turning left when it meets another road. Now you should spot the church in the near distance, so walk on just a little further before turning right down a small unnamed road to the pub, where a delicious lunch and a cool drink awaits.

History

Just east of St Kenelm's church you will spot a mediaeval barn, which was built for Winchcombe Abbey, a Benedictine monastery that once owned the manor of Enstone.

Its date stone reads 1382, but the manner of the barn's construction suggests it is a late 15th building. Historians believe that the barn may have been rebuilt, but the date stone from an earlier structure retained.

Eynsham
The Red Lion

The Red Lion, Eynsham, is the oldest pub in the village, so it has earned its prominent place in the village square. Eynsham, where Pythius and I live, is just south of the A40 between Oxford and Witney.

Its close neighbours include the 13th century parish church of St Leonard's, also the 18th century Bartholomew Room that began life as a place to educate local boys. A splendid hand carved copy of the original village cross that dated back to the 14th century can be found in the square too.

During the January snows that kept us all within the confines of the village for 10 days, Auntie Liz, Pythius and I visited the Red Lion several times. (Pythius gets withdrawal symptoms if he doesn't put his paws under a pub table at least once a week).

This pub has two faces. During the morning it attracts a few locals who happily prop up the bar, enjoying a glass or two of real ale. In the evening, the youngsters take over.

We called during lunch time, contenting ourselves with a glass of Old Speckled Hen and a bag of crisps, as staff who normally run the kitchen were unable to travel to the village. When the snow began to thaw we were able to treat ourselves to a plate of cod and chips to go with the beer.

Pythius Says

I guess I am really lucky dog as there are loads of pubs in my village and several allow me in. The Red Lion is particularly dog-friendly and I often find myself in the company of other canines when we pop in for a drink.

Obviously I know all the walks round Eynsham very well as this is where I live and am one of those lucky dogs who gets two walks a day. We take the Pink Hill Lane walk when it's a nice day and when Helen wants to enjoy the feeling of space that these fields offer her. We sometimes run these fields early in the morning, as the garage that services her little Mini is on the nearby industrial estate. If the Mini only needs a small job to fix it, Helen often takes me with her, then we walk the Pink Hill Lane and its fields instead of waiting in Mr Bruno's office. As the Mini continues to grow older and older, such visits are becoming more frequent, but Helen loves her scruffy little car so much she won't give up on it. She calls it her mobile dog kennel, but I have never worked out why.

Yes, the food served here is basic pub grub, it doesn't pretend to be anything else, but that's fine. It is nicely cooked and always served with a smile.

We enjoy the convivial atmosphere generated by chattering locals and those who tuck themselves into a corner while hugging their pint and relaxing with a newspaper.

Actually the Red Lion offers everything you would expect from a village pub that stands in the very centre of the village. In the 1950s it was said to be the only place where the game of Ttipit was played – this is a hunt-the-slipper type of game played with an old threepenny bit. It was also the domino and cribbage centre of the village and the headquarters of the Eynsham football and cricket clubs for many years.

The Walk

Leave the pub and turn right towards the main road that runs through the village, and right again past the newsagents and on towards the playing fields that are found just four minutes walk away on the right hand side of the road. Walk across the playing fields, heading for the Chil Brook that acts as a boundary and flows at the bottom of the field, and then for the little foot bridge in the far left hand corner that leads to the very busy B4044. Do take care to control your dog at this point, keeping him firmly fixed to his lead, as this road attracts speeding cars.

Almost opposite this exit you will spot a footpath sign which leads though a kissing gate and into a small field often occupied by cows. A well-worn path across the grass takes you diagonally towards another kissing gate on the left hand side.

You are now free to let the dog off the lead and walk through three further fields, and on towards Pinkhill Lane.

Very few cars travel this lane, so I tend to let Pythius wander free, but under close control. This lane leads to a farm if you turn left, but if you turn right it eventually takes you to the Station Road and a roundabout. Turn right at the roundabout and you will soon find yourself back to the footbridge you originally crossed at the corner of the playing fields.

This walk will take you about an hour from start to finish. I must admit it offered some rare treats for Pythius when it was covered in snow.

History

May I advise all visitors to pick up a copy of *Eynsham Unlocked*, a free brochure giving details of the many interesting buildings that you will find in this historic village. Most local shops have copies available.

Because there was a Benedictine abbey founded in Eynsham in 1005, which was surrendered to Henry VIII in 1539, many of the abbey stones were eventually used to build many of the cottages you see today. You might well enjoy trying to work out which buildings owe their existence to abbey stones, when walking the village.

If you approach Eynsham from Oxford on the B4044 you will be asked to pay 5 pence if you wish to cross the 18th century toll bridge at Swinford by car. It's said that this is due to King George III whose coach crossed the ford towards Eynsham at a time when the river Thames was high and his carriage almost foundered. By Act of Parliament, the king grated Lord Abingdon the right to build a bridge over the ford and charge a toll. It was opened in 1769. The takings, then, as now, are tax free. The bridge sold at auction for £1.08m in 2009.

Fairford
The Bull Hotel

There were originally more than 20 pubs, inns and ale-houses in Fairford as this attractive Cotswold market town was the transport centre for stagecoaches on the long-distance routes between London and Gloucester, Oxford and Bristol. It also stood on the ancient droving route known as the Welsh Way (now the A417 between Cirencester and Lechlade) on which livestock were driven to London markets. There are only five pubs in Fairford now. The one we always use is The Bull Hotel which dominates the market square; it is such a friendly place to relax and dogs are always welcome in the large beamed bar.

It's thought to date from the 15th century when it used to be a monks' changing house. By the 18th century it had become a popular posting house with stables for 30 horses. When building work took place recently, a secret tunnel was discovered leading from the hotel to St Mary's Church that also dates to the 15th century and stands but a stone's throw away. The moment you walk through the door a sense of its great history engulfs you – it is that kind of place.

As this is an Arkell's pub which stocks the full range of Arkell's beers, there is plenty of real ale to choose from, including the award-winning 3B, a best bitter first brewed in 1910 and known by many as a 'Big Boy's Beer'.

I have always liked the fact that this atmospheric hotel will happily supply you with a packed lunch if you fancy a picnic during your riverside walk. If you want to eat in-house, the bar menu is extensive. I defy anyone to walk away disappointed, having viewed the many dishes listed on the large blackboard menu close to the bar. There really is something for everyone and at a reasonable price. Despite always attracting a good crowd during the lunch period, food is usually

served promptly and with a warm smile that suggests a real welcome.

The Walk

Finding the river walk once you have left the pub couldn't be easier; turn right on leaving the pub and cross the A417 that runs through the town and step into Back Lane, which is signed as a river walk. This leads to Gas Lane and then the River Coln. At this point the river is not deep, which makes it an ideal place for dogs to splash about and enjoy

---

Pythius says

What a pub – what a walk! A dog's delight in every way. The pub is friendly, although it does tend to get very busy at times and I have to watch where I place my paws in case someone steps on them. But the staff are really kindly; they kept patting me on the head and calling me love, which was all rather nice.

As for the walk, well what can I possibly say? It's river, river, river all the way, and such a lovely river. Not too deep, not at all muddy and the water is so clear and crisp, a dog could ask for nothing better. The other good thing about this walk if you simply follow the river until it's time to turn back, is that you simply can't get lost, a big plus when walking with Helen and Auntie Liz who are inclined to lose their way from time to time. What more can I say? A perfect walk – a perfect day.

themselves. Pythius certainly loves this river, which he has enjoyed in Chedworth, Bibury and Coln St Aldwyns and several small villages in between as it journeys from the Cotswold Hills to Lechlade where it joins the Thames. The river is host to many species of freshwater fish including brown trout and grayling and attracts a considerable number of kingfishers. It is indeed a beautiful river.

The last time we took this walk we simply ambled along the river bank, stopping now and again to enjoy the views and listen to the gentle ripples of the water making its way over a pebbled bed. Had we wished, we could have followed the river to a series of water meadows, eventually reaching a footbridge which gives access to the banks of a large lake. As it was a hot day, we walked about three quarters of a mile, and then ambled back again, stopping to sit by the river under a shady tree when it got too hot. It really is a lovely walk, for both humans and dogs. Serious walkers can continue to Lechlade if they wish to walk at least six miles there and six miles back again. Auntie Liz, Pythius and I are not serious walkers!

History

No other town in the country boasts such a superb near-complete set of original medieval stained glass windows as those found in St Mary's Church, Fairford.

The 28 windows in this church date back nearly 500 years. The glass was made between 1500 and 1517 under the direction of the King's glazier, Barnard Flower, in his Westminster workshops.

These brightly coloured windows are arranged to a carefully planned scheme that includes episodes from the life of Christ and illustrations of the prophets, apostles and teachers of the faith. You will not regret taking a moment to view them.

Fringford
The Butcher's Arms

Uncle John and I decided to take a few steps back in time and take Pythius to Juniper Hill, the hamlet that stands in a remote rural corner where Oxfordshire, Northamptonshire and Buckinghamshire meet. This is the place that Flora Thompson brought to life in her classic semi-autobiogaphical *Lark Rise to Candleford*, which describes Oxfordshire life in a farming community during the late 19th century.

We decided to visit the nearby villages of Fringford and Cottisford too, as they both featured large in her life.

Lark Rise was Flora's fictional name for Juniper Hill. The village of Fringford, where she worked as a Post Office assistant from 1891 to 1897, she named Candleford Green. The village of Cottisford where she went to school throughout the week and church on Sundays, she called Fordlow. All three can be found about four miles north of Bicester.

Unfortunately the Fox Inn that Flora's father used to frequent, that once dominated the small cluster of houses that make up Juniper Hill, is no more. It was converted to a private residence many years ago. So to turn this into a pub walk, we had to visit The Butcher's Arms, Fringford instead. But that was fine as it stands in the centre of Fringford, and close to the building which was once the Post Office.

This 17th century ivy-clad pub, which stands next to the village green, offers everything you expect of a traditional village pub. Uncle John and Pythius stood by the entrance when we arrived, while I went in to ask if a dog would be welcome. After looking around the bar area, the woman who was to serve us pointed to a table in the far corner by the piano. "There are two black Labradors sitting the other side, but you are very welcome to sit over there," she said. Happiness is finding a pub that accepts that dogs are as entitled as their owners to a comfortable place in the pub and we had obviously found such a pub.

The lunch menu features the most amazing assortment of reasonably priced sandwiches, baguettes and filled ciabattas, and when I say filled, I do mean filled with a capital F. My scrumptious bacon sandwich in French bread contained three thick slices of crunchy bacon and Uncle John's ham sandwich was so generously stuffed with ham, he struggled to finish it.

The range of real ales proved impressive too. We went for Adnam's Broadside, which hit the spot nicely, but there were several others to choose from. The large array of sporting trophies on display, the dart board and the pub's close proximity to the cricket field suggested that this pub remains the village meeting place, just as it would have been in Flora's time.

We loved the buzzing atmosphere, the sparkling horse brasses, the dark-wood panelled walls and the friendly nature of the bar staff. Nothing was too much trouble and we were certainly made welcome even though we arrived at the tail end of the lunch period. We left feeling that this pub was as much a piece of social history as Flora's books.

The Walk

The Butchers Arms is about two miles from Cottisford, where we started our walk to Juniper Hill. Whilst we could have walked there, it would have added four miles along tarmac roads to our day, so we took the lazy way out and covered the distance by car.

Parking at Cottisford is difficult. We ended up by tucking our car tight onto a grass verge close to St Mary's Church, where Flora worshipped. The school she attended stands in this village too, though it closed in 1973 and is now a domestic residence.

We began the day by admiring the church that Flora Thompson described in *Lark Rise*. In her words 'it is a tiny place about the size of a barn with nave and chancel only, no side aisles, with a tiny church-yard that centuries of use had raised many feet above the ground.' It was all very atmospheric.

Leaving the church we turned left and walked about 100 yards along the road until we reached the waymarker on the left hand side pointing to Juniper Hill. This took us through a hedge and into a large field.

There's a little brook running alongside this field and Pythius did eventually manage to find a way through the dense foliage strip besides it, but the water didn't seem to satisfy him. It smelt stale and there was a considerable amount of algae covering the surface.

In Memoriam
FLORA THOMPSON
1876 - 1947
Born Flora Jane Timms
at Juniper Hill
she worshipped here as a child
before moving to Fringford
Author of
"Lark Rise To Candleford"

The wild strip besides the

Pythius says

I am never happy when the promised walk starts with a church visit, but have to admit it proved a happy little place with loads of interesting smells in the churchyard.

On reaching the first field it soon became apparent this was not going to be one of those wonderful walks where I could run free. The path between the brook and the field proved far too narrow to do anything but walk forward and follow a well-worn path and the brook proved a disappointment. When I finally found a way down the bank I soon realised this was not going to be a joyful experience. The water was covered with green stuff and actually smelt rather rank. Bad smells normally attract me, but not this time. I jumped out as quickly as I had jumped in and dutifully followed Helen and Uncle John as they walked the narrow path between the corn and the wild flowers and grasses.

I admit being slightly alarmed to discover a rusting metal animal trap half covered by vegetation along the way – it was too old to have been in working condition, but alarming nevertheless.

The second cornfield was easier, there was a healthy feeling of space as we ambled along a well worn track right through the centre as we made our way towards the little wooden stile which seemed to intrigue Helen and Uncle John so much that they spent a long time stroking the wood and admiring its simple shape. (They are easily pleased at times!)

When they noticed the horses in the next area I was immediately put onto my lead which was boring. I was kept on my lead as we travelled to the writer-lady's house too. Tedious!

I still don't know what all the fuss was about, because we didn't even go into the house once we had found it. However, the sun was shining, there were some wonderful smells and aromas for me to enjoy, and Helen and Uncle John seemed happy to have reached their destination – so who was I to complain? I'm learning to be quite philosophical about such things these days.

As to the pub, well that's a different story. What a friendly place it proved to be. I loved it and would have happily joined the two black Labradors for a chat if I had been allowed to. I wasn't. Paws had to be kept firmly under the table.

Because Helen was conscious I hadn't had many wild runs during this walk, she took me onto the village green and cricket ground next to the pub once lunch was finished.

That proved a great mistake. I was in full flight, having a wonderful time as Uncle John threw my ball when a young man marched purposefully towards us. Gosh Helen was in trouble! She hadn't spotted a sign to the right of the green stating that dogs were not permitted to run on the grass. He explained that the village was very proud of their green and didn't want dogs spoiling it. Uncle John picked up the ball, Helen placed me back on my lead and we made our way back to the pub car park, hanging our heads in shame.

stream may have been tangled and wild, but it certainly attracts an amazing number of butterflies which delighted Uncle John who is now coming up with some amazing close-up shots of flora and fauna with his new camera.

We disturbed several pheasants lurking amongst the stems of corn as we journed along the footpath, and were lucky enough to see a flock of swallows preparing for their long trip back to Africa.

Once we'd walked along the left side of the first corn field and travelled the path through the middle of the second, we reached the old wooden style that Flora Thompson used when making this mile journey from her home to the church.

Despite its age, it's a sturdy little stile that proved easy to climb with room for Pythius to pass through too. Now Jupiter Hill comes into view as you travel a well-kept green path, with vegetable plots on the left and horses on the right. As this path leads to the main road that runs through the village, it's best to put the dog on its lead at this point, for although the timeless nature of this amazing little place will have seduced you into thinking you are in a time warp, cars travel this road frequently. Besides, whilst the horses could not get out of their enclosure, dogs can get in and horses and dogs don't always mix.

At the metal gate and the road, we turned left and ambled towards the sign saying Juniper Hill, then turned into the first pathway to the left. We

had reached the place that Flora described as the hamlet that stood on a gentle rise in the flat wheat-growing north-east corner of Oxfordshire. She goes on to say that to a passer-by on the main road, it must often have appeared a lone and desolate place, but a closer observer would have found it as seething with interest and activity as a molehill.

The house in which Flora Thompson spent her childhood is reached by walking past several attractive little cottages and following a green path that winds to the right. Her original home has been altered since her day with several extensions added, and the thatch roof has been replaced with slate. A sign asks visitors not to walk onto the gravel drive as it is private property, so our photograph is taken from the road

and only show the side of this white-washed house.

Having explored a little further, we returned to Cottisford the way we had come. The walk there and back took us about an hour because we took our time, stopping now and again to absorb the atmosphere. But as it is only two miles in total, it can be walked in far less if you don't allow you imagination to flow back to Flora's day, when the landscape would have been busy with men and horses working the fields.

Back in Cottisford, we drove the two miles to Fringford and the Butchers Arms which is well sign posted.

History

For the most comprehensive history of this region it's worth reading Martin Greenwood's excellent book *In Flora's Footsteps*. In his conclusion he writes: "The story of these villages is like an ever-flowing stream in which we all swim for a brief while. As we have seen, much has changed but, as all local historians love to say, there is much evidence too of continuity."

Hailey
The Lamb and Flag

Hailey stands on the south-eastern edge of the old Wychwood Forest and just a couple of miles from Witney. You will find the Lamb and Flag on the B4022 that runs through the village. There were three pubs in Hailey once, now only the Lamb and Flag remains.

The worn flagstones in the main bar area bear witness to the countless feet that have walked into this homely little 17th century pub over the years. The many photographs of cricket and football teams that have used this pub – some dating back to 1929 – suggest it has served the community for some considerable time. And the highly polished furnishings and gleaming horse brasses that adore the large stone fireplace suggest the current licensee takes pride in its appearance.

Auntie Liz and I had not intended to visit this pub, we had planned to visit Wolvercote and the Godstow Nunnery ruins, but all four pubs in the area refused Pythius entrance. As it was far too cold to sit outside, we made our way to Hailey instead and were very glad we did.

Not only was Pythius made welcome, Tom the barman actually remembered us, even though several years have passed since my previous visit.

One of the great things about this pub is that everything is home cooked, the vegetables follow the seasons and the portions are generous. Minted lamb pie, grilled trout and home made curries feature on the menu at very reasonable prices.

It's a Greene King pub and unfortunately the choice of real ales is limited, but the beers that are offered are well kept. No doubt the hard working Tom keeps the lines clean and cared for.

While enjoying our lunch we made conversation with Keith, one of the many regulars who call in at lunchtime for a companionable pint. It was Keith who told us that the pub may be haunted by a crying baby, and who then went on to describe a walk we could take to the newly established Community Woodland nearby, which was created in 2003 as one of Oxfordshire's Golden Jubilee Wildlife Spaces..

The Walk

This walk couldn't be easier. Having asked permission, we left the car in the Lamb and Flag's car park and with our back to the pub, we turned left, walking about 150 yards through the area known as Middletown until we spotted a little red pillar box and a waymarker pointing left to the Community Woodland.

Now it is just a matter of walking the little tree lined lane. You will encounter a couple of stiles on each side of the lane after about 100 yards, but ignore these and carry on until you finally reach another Community Woodland sign pointing left.

The main species of trees within this delightful little wood are oak and ash as they reflect the species found within the forest of Wychwood. The shrubs used around the margins and in the hedges are native and local species. There are hazel coppices too, which are there for production of thatching spars and hedge laying materials. Rides are sown with a pollen and nectar mix to encourage butterflies, bees and insects.

Should you wish, you can walk through the woodland and take another path leading to Whitings Lane. This will take you back to Hailey, but as this is a tarmac route and dogs will have to be kept on the lead, it is best to enjoy the woodland, walking round and through the trees until the dog is worn out, and then return the way you came.

> *Pythius says:*
>
> Some pubs feel welcoming the moment you enter. The Lamb and Flag certainly did. I admit being very flattered to find that the nice barman Tom gave me a pat on the head as soon as I came in the front door – he seemed to consider me a very important customer.
>
> The locals who talked to us were kindly too. In other words – a great little pub that I would like to visit often.
>
> And the walk? Oh that was fine, no streams or rivers to splash about in, but loads of lovely earthy smells and badgers setts to investigate along the way. I could tell that lots of dogs walk this area and enjoy the walk just as I did.

We spent about an hour, enjoying both the lane and the woodlands and noting the large badger setts along the way. Pythius loved this walk as he was able to walk free the moment we entered the lane.

History

Some might say that Hailey is of no historical importance and that it has always lived on edge of history, however John Wesley made frequent visits to this area and it is thought that Priest Hill Lane was named in his honour.

The village is divided into three parts: Delly End, Middletown and Poffley End which takes its name from poffle, a 14th century word used to denote a small parcel of land that often tapers to a point.

As its name suggests Middletown, links the villages. The name Hailey is thought to come from the local practice of stacking hay into leys, hence Hayley and then Hailey.

Hook Norton
The Pear Tree Inn

Visitors are aware that they are approaching the rural north Oxfordshire village of Hook Norton (signed off the A361 between Chipping Norton and Banbury) when they see the road signs decorated with little brown beer barrels. They will know they have arrived when an aromatic fragrance of roasted malt begins to tantalise their nostrils.

Although Hook Norton's Victorian brewery stands on the northern edge of the village, its presence dominates the area. The aromas from its brews begin permeating the air the moment that the brewery's ancient steam engine begins pumping water from the well and the malt is crushed in the grist mill at 6am.

There are three Hook Norton pubs in the village; we always use the Pear Tree Inn, which stands next to Brewer Lane (which – as its name suggests – leads to the brewery).

Dogs are not allowed inside the brewery's visitor centre, but I often walk Pythius up the lane just so that we can stand and stare at this magnificent ironstone building. It always amuses me to watch Pythius's nose twitch as the malt aroma gets more and more intense. As I have often remarked, whilst he is not allowed to drink beer, I can't stop him enjoying its malty aroma.

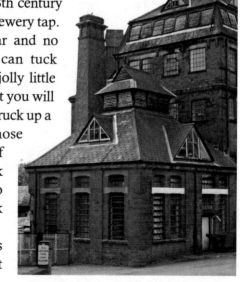

The Pear Tree is a pretty 18th century pub which also serves as the brewery tap. Because there is only one bar and no other rooms where visitors can tuck themselves away, it is a very jolly little pub. You might go in alone, but you will seldom leave without having struck up a conversation or two with those congregated around the bar. Of course the full range of Hook Norton Beers are available, so real ale lovers are never stuck for choice.

The first time Pythius walked in he was somewhat

alarmed to note a magnificent Airedale dog marching around the tables as if he owned the place.

Well, he might not own it, but it's certainly his home. His name is King and he was found abandoned by Ian Miller, the licensee, who decided to give him a home. Ian did such a good job of restoring King to his full glory that he became a winner at Crufts. Once Pythius learned that, he gave King the respect he deserved and they became friends.

Polly the black Labrador and his lovely mistress, Kate the volunteer Cotswold warden, joined us the last time we visited the Pear Tree Inn. We called for lunch having enjoyed a three-and-a-half mile circular walk on a sunny autumn day. Had there been a nip in the air the log fire would have been roaring away to add extra cheer, but the day was far too warm for a fire.

Once the dogs had settled themselves under the table, having said hello to King, Kate and I tucked into a home cooked fish and chip lunch, which we washed down with a couple of half pints of Old Hooky that hit the spot perfectly. Don't expect anything posh at this friendly little pub, the food is basic pub fare, but that said it is as good as anything you will find in the area. If the steak and Hooky pie is on the menu, that's certainly worth ordering, but as its so popular it sells out quickly.

Because the Pear Tree Inn opens all day, it's the perfect place to head for after a walk.

The Walk

Turn left after leaving the pub and head towards the church, and then turn right into Middle Hill, which links with Park Road. You need to cross a small bridge which may be covered with so much foliage it is hardly visible, so look out for a small red pillar box and a wooden bench and turn left at that point.

Continue walking, keeping a row of bungalows on your left until you come to a waymarker on the right which takes you out of Hook Norton and towards the tall ivy-clad remains of the old railway viaduct, which once carried Great Western trains across the valley. All railway traffic passing this way was stopped in 1964 leaving just seven magnificent pillars that are gently decaying, relying on the ivy to keep them upright.

You are now walking a well worn path that will take you past Park Farm on the left and horses in the right-hand field. You soon reach a small wooded area and a metal gate.

If you reach the ford, you have gone too far and should head left up the bank and through the trees to a field and a well-worn track. Once again just follow the footpath, keeping trees to your right.

On reaching a small bridge spanning a little stream you will notice Manor Farm on your left, where a large herd of very contented cows often sit somnolently under the trees. Put your dog on the lead and

---

Pythius Says

We often come to Hook Norton (affectionately named Hooky by those who live here).

It's a really pretty village and that glorious malty smell really gets my taste buds going. Sometimes we walk up to the old brewery, stand and stare for a moment or two, then take a footpath on the right hand side by a farm gate.

That walk is OK, but I like the Manor Farm walk better, providing Helen stays calm when she spots the cows and watches out for the safe place to cross the electric fence. As for the pub, well now I have made friends with King, all is fine. It's a warm friendly room, with hops hanging from the beams. As dogs are allowed to sit anywhere there is space for them I always feel welcome. Water is in a bowl by the front door. Polly and I had lots to talk about by the way, as she has lost loads of weight since last year – gosh she is a really slim-line dog now and now looks so beautiful I found myself chatting her up.

walk carefully towards the farm buildings, climbing over an electric fence at the end, which has a safe spot covered with rubber tubing for walkers to pass without being given an electric shock. Waymarkers can be seen on farm buildings directing you on a small path between the two barns.

Follow this into a track leading to a tangled woody area and a clapped out wooden bridge that takes you back over the stream. From here on it's dead easy as the path leading back to Hook Norton is well marked and fenced off in parts. Just be careful when you spot the next electric fence, as the safe crossing point covered with tubing may not be easy to spot.

After passing a couple of fields of sheep you will notice the distant church tower emerging majestically through the trees.

This walk took us a couple of hours because we ambled and spent time letting Polly and Pythius splash about in the stream. Kate also had problems with me when I spotted the cows. She kindly took time out to look for another route, before leading me safely through the herd as only Kate can. Gosh she is a remarkable friend, no one else I know understands the countryside as she does.

History

When the farmer and maltster John Harris set up his brewery in a Hook Norton farm house more than 150 years ago, most towns and villages could boast their own brewery. Now very few family breweries remain and the Hook Norton Bewery has become a working museum with a string of award-winning brews to its name.

The gleaming 25hp steam engine, which still drives the essential parts of machinery used in the brewery, just as it did more than 100 years ago, is perhaps the most remarkable survivor.

The brewery's Visitor Centre, which opened in 1990, is the starting point for brewery tours that incorporate the sight of the engine. These tours take place every day but Sunday.

Islip
The Swan

If you are looking for a pub and a village that oozes with historical interest, Islip is certainly the place for you. Now a mile from the A34 north of Oxford, its history is shaped by Edward the Confessor's birth in the village around 1005 and later the Civil War, when Cromwell won the Battle of Islip. But that's not all it is famous for, which is why a visit is necessary to absorb the atmosphere of this charming little place, visit its ancient church, and walk the streets in which the poet Robert Graves walked when he lived here from 1921 to 1925.

But first you need liquid refreshment and a good hearty home-cooked meal, which you can enjoy at The Swan, which stands a stone's throw from Islip's famous bridge.

This delightful little village pub is thought to date back to the 18th century, though it could be older. There's nothing fancy or modern about this pub. In fact when you walk through the main door you would be forgiven for thinking you have already taken a step back in time. I have been visiting the Swan for at least 20 years, and it seems that nothing has changed since I first walked in with my beloved dog Apollo, who died more than 12 years ago.

Dogs are still welcome. Actually they are very welcome. On asking if Pythius would be allowed in, I was immediately asked if he liked 'gravy biscuits', as they were always available for dogs who bring their masters in for a meal. Water is on hand for canine visitors too.

Thanks to the very friendly and informative barmaid Megan, a farmer's daughter who lives at Manor Farm down the road and has three dogs of her own, Pythius felt at home immediately, and we were given lots of information about the village and its history. From the way Megan spoke, it sounded as if she knew every field and blade of grass in the village. She certainly knew every walk. It's the existence of hard-working women like Megan, who are prepared to run the extra mile to ensure that customers are happy, that makes village pubs such a joy to visit. Nothing was too much trouble and everything was seasoned with a generous serving of good old fashioned hospitality.

The menu is basic, but as it includes a very reasonably priced list of sandwiches that come with chips and salad, as well as classic dishes such as cottage or shepherd's pie, it offered everything we needed the day we called.

There is a small restaurant area to the left of the bar, but Auntie Liz and I stayed in the bar, sipping our Greene King ale and munching on a freshly cooked shepherd's pie.

There is a large car park opposite the pub and standing alongside the river and the bridge, so parking is not a problem. We were given permission to leave the car there when we embarked on the Confessor's Walk.

The Walk

Should you wish, you can walk the towpath along the River Cherwell all the way to Oxford, if you turn left on reaching the river. But we decided to walk the newly established Confessor's Way, which circles the village. This commemorative walk, which opened in June 2006, celebrates the birth of Edward the Confessor, which the village marked throughout 2005.

You can begin the walk at the church or the village community shop, as you will find waymarkers throughout the village, but we began the walk from the pub, which means we walked it the wrong way round. That doesn't matter; it just means that when you see a waymarker pointing left you go right. As the walk is very well marked, I doubt that anyone could get lost regardless of which way they walk it, as even Auntie Liz and I managed it without a mistake!

We headed for the Islip bridge, the site of the Civil War battle, which is straight ahead, and crossed it. Do be careful at this point as the traffic can be quite fast along this road (B4027) and there is very little room for walkers and their dogs. It's best to keep the dog tight to your side. Once over the bridge you can relax. You will face two lanes on the right hand

Pythius says

I am always rather wary when Auntie Liz and Helen get excited about all things historical. I want to say: "Hey you two, dogs don't care about dates and all that stuff, we just go by the smells," but I usually just let them chatter on, while I enjoy sniffing out history in my own way.

The pub, for example, smelt good the moment I walked in. I knew it would be a happy place and it was. I was offered a gravy biscuit the moment I arrived, but spoilsport Helen told that lovely Megan I don't eat between meals. So I had to make do with water and a pat on the head while they munched their way through a delicious home-cooked meal. Sometimes life isn't fair if you are a dog.

Obviously things perked up when we crossed the bridge and began the walk, which took us straight over a very large field to the river. I would have liked to have run round the field and enjoy the space, but a winter crop had been planted there, so I had to follow Auntie Liz and Helen along the path until we reached the river where we had lots of fun. They stopped and listened to the birdsong, while I jumped in and out of the water chasing my ball – well balls actually, as I let the fast-moving current wash the first one away. Then I discovered a plastic bottle on the bank which was far more interesting. I adore plastic bottles, as they make the most delicious crunchy noise when I bite into them.

Inspecting the church was tedious, but as this happened towards the end of the walk, I didn't complain.

side. Take Bridge Street, keeping a couple of cottages on your left hand side, walk up the lane bearing left and on to the village allotments and the millennium woods. You will finally reach a gap and a large field that is usually planted up with wheat. Here you will find a way sign for the Confessor's Walk pointing in the opposite direction. You will also notice a well-walked path passing diagonally through the field towards the river. Once you have crossed this path and reached the edge of the field, there is a gap and another waymarker. At this point turn right to the river Cherwell, and on reaching its bank, turn right again until you reach the weir and a metal bridge. As you cross this bridge you will notice that this is the point where the River Ray meets the River Cherwell. Even during the winter months, this is a very beautiful spot with an abundance of birds and wild life.

Cross the bridge at the weir, then turn right following a short green path to a metal gate. At this point you will notice two 30 mph signs, which indicates a road. Put your dog on the lead now, as you have reached Mill Street.

Half way up this street, you will find another way sign directing you left over the village playing field and on to the village shop and a children's playground, where two large carved wooden figures that appear to depict Edward the Confessor stand proud and tall.

The village shop is small and run by volunteers, but it is such a friendly place, it is well worth a visit. It's here that you can buy a copy of *Islip, Oxfordshire*, a very informative and well illustrated little book compiled by the Islip History group. From the shop and its car park, turn right until you reach St Edward's Church. Take the stone steps that lead to the church and churchyard, stopping for a moment to admire the interior of this historic building, before carrying on until you reach Mill Street again. At this point turn left and within moments you will find yourself back at the Swan's car park.

I guess we walked about a mile, certainly no more, though naturally Pythius ran about five miles as he darted backwards and forwards along the riverbank having the time of his life.

History

Because of its strategic location, armies have passed through Islip and troops have been garrisoned in the village at times of crisis – most particularly during the Civil War. There was a Royal Garrison at Islip in 1645 as Cromwell advanced with 1500 dragoons from Watlington. Cromwell launched his main attack from the south and down the hill towards the bridge. His guns on high ground put the royalist forces at a great disadvantage and the bridge was taken, with fighting continuing through the streets of Islip. It is thought that Cromwell spent the night in Islip after the battle and various claims exist as to the exact location of his lodgings.

Long Wittenham
The Plough Inn

There's Long Wittenham and Little Wittenham, but only Long Wittenham has a pub. This means we usually stop off at The Plough when in the area, then travel a couple of miles in the car to Little Wittenham and the historic Wittenham Clumps to walk the dog.

Long Wittenham stands on the south bank of the Thames, about a couple of miles from both Didcot and Wallingford.

It's a tranquil little village with a history that stretches way back through the centuries, as the vast variety of architectural styles within the village testify, despite the fact that many buildings were destroyed in a devastating fire that swept through it during 1868. Long Wittenham even has a cruck cottage which is believed to be at least 800 years old, and therefore one of the oldest in the country.

The imposing red brick Plough Inn, which was established as a pub in 1861, stands on the High Street at the far end of the village, close to the famed Pendon Indoor Model Village and Railway Museum.

It's here at the Plough Inn, with its massive garden abutting the Thames, that the red-coated swan uppers stop for lunch as they make their annual summer journey up the Thames from Cookham to Abingdon, checking and counting the swans and cygnets they encounter along the way. This historic ceremony, which takes place during the third week in July, dates from the 12th century when the crown claimed ownership of all mute swans.

If you enjoy homely unspoiled pubs that put hospitality first, you will love the Plough. Its rooms are small and unspoiled by modern design trends and the staff who have worked together for many years clearly enjoy their jobs.

It goes without saying that the food

Pythius Says

There's a kindly barman at the Plough called Don who always makes a real fuss of me when we visit this pub. He's a really jolly person who never fails to make us welcome. I love this pub and always feel comfortable when we visit.

As to the walk to the top of Castle Hill, then round and round the top – well in many ways it is absolutely fantastic, but I have finally worked out why I feel so exhausted at the end of the walk. It's all those balls that Helen and Auntie Liz thrown down the path for me to chase. Well, following the ball down the slope is fine for a while, it's also fun rushing up the hill again with the ball in my mouth. But (yes there is a but) there comes a moment when Helen throws down just one ball too many.

Thank goodness the girls stop when they get to the top and sit on one of the many benches arranged around the clump to admire the view. This gives me a chance to save face and catch my breath before we go round and round the top and then down again. It wouldn't do for them to discover that even border collies can get tired occasionally.

They sometimes stop for a moment to read the poem etched on the Poem Tree too – they find this fascinating but I just see it as another chance to rest.

is reasonably priced hearty pub fare and the range of real ales on offer impressive. I love this pub.

The Walk

Before leaving for Wittenham Clumps it's worth walking to St Mary's Church, which you will find just down the road if you turn left after leaving the Plough Inn.

Built about 1120, with later additions and with a with a superb timber porch which is said to have come from Lincoln Cathedral, it's here that you will discover a remarkable lead font, one of only three such fonts in the country. Dating back to the 12th century and embossed with decorative discs and 30 little archbishops, it was encased in wood during the Civil War to prevent Roundhead soldiers melting it down for bullets. Apparently its wood casing was not removed and its full beauty exposed again until 1839.

Little Wittenham is well signposted and easy to find; besides, as this area is mostly flat you really can't miss the Clumps topped with trees as these ancient hill forts stand tall and proud and can be viewed from many vantage points. From Long Wittenham , head north east along High Street, turning right at the Little Wittenham Road and bearing right when you reach this village as the car park to the reserves is just a half a mile or so along the road. You can't miss it.

Once you have parked your car, where you walk is up to you. You will find clear informative maps mounted at most gates to the area by the Northmoor Trust who manage this superb 250 acre nature reserve, which is a Site of Special Scientific Interest.

The main thing you have to watch for when arriving with a dog are the sheep that graze this area. As they are constantly moved from one patch to another, it's a matter of spotting where they are and then honouring the Trust's request to keep your dog under control when near livestock.

From the car park you will see Castle Hill immediately as it stands majestically before you, urging you forward. The second clump (Round Hill) stands further to the left.

My favourite trick having reached the top of Castle Hill is to throw Pythius's ball down to the bottom. Poor little fellow bounds down after it with great enthusiasm and returns panting, with the ball stuck firmly between his teeth. It only takes a half a dozen throws like that to exhaust him totally, such that he finally gives up and simply ambles beside us for the rest of the walk, stopping now and again as we do for a well earned rest.

Strategically placed seats on the top of both clumps offer walkers a chance to sit and enjoy the views, while they listen to the skylarks and yellowhammers who fill the air with their song during the summer months.

The view is stunning as you are presented with a different scene at every turn. There's the picturesque view of the lowlands across to the Berkshire Downs to the south. Walk in a south westerly direction and you will see the massive Didcot Power Station chimneys. Then there's the historic riverside town of Dorchester nestling in a fold of the Thames when you turn again.

Within the Northmoor Trust Estate there are also wetland areas, woods and an arboretum, making it a walker's paradise – but do watch out for those grazing sheep and ground nesting birds.

History

While wandering around the Castle Hill clump you will discover the trunk of a dead tree on which words appear to have been cut into the bark with a knife. The tree died in the early 1990s and unfortunately the words are now really difficult to read. But all is not lost – beside this

tree trunk stands a large plaque on which the original poem, carved in 1844/1845 by Joseph Tubb of Warborough Green, has been transcribed.

Thanks to Dr Henry Osmaston, who took an accurate tracing of the poem in 1965 while the tree was still alive and the words were much more legible, visitors are able to read the poem which describes the scene laid out before them. The plaque commemorates the 150th anniversary of the poem.

Longworth
The Blue Boar

There's something quite magical about the aroma of woodsmoke, particularly when it hits the nostrils the moment you have left your car and prepare to walk into a country pub. It not only suggests warmth, but conviviality too.

You can't miss the massive log fire at the Blue Boar, Tucks Lane, Longworth. It's right by the bar and so close to the main door that its heat hits you as soon as you walk in. Almost everyone who enters on a cold winter's day stops to admire it and warm themselves before giving their order – however, few stay too close as the heat it gives out is awesome.

Pythius and I do enjoy visiting this 17th century thatched, ivy-clad pub, which is thought to have started life as a bakery and an Elizabethan ale house. During the 19th century it became a stopping place for drovers.

It has never once disappointed me as it offers everything I could possibly ask for, including a great blackboard menu and an excellent choice of real ales, wooden scrubbed tables and benches, and efficient, friendly service. The dried hops that decorate the beams and the many copper kettles and ornaments scattered around the bar add their own special touch. Dogs are always welcome here, and are treated with the respect that they deserve.

This pub became so popular that an extension was built a couple of years ago to accommodate the many walkers who frequent this area,. To find it, take the A415 north (towards Witney) from a roundabout on the A420 between Oxford and Faringdon.

Longworth is one of a chain of villages that lies on a ridge of fertile, fast-draining loam that runs north as far as Oxford, known as the Golden ridge. During the 18th century this terrain gave farmers a strong advantage as their crops were more bountiful than those of their less favoured neighbours. In the 19th century the rose arrived, thanks to five families of nurserymen who found ideal soil conditions in the area and a captive market due to the farmers' prosperity. During the next 175 years, their names became synonyms for the best British rose growing. Sadly only the name Mattock exists now. Robert Mattock continues to produce ravishing containerised roses in nearby Abingdon, which always take pride of place in the annual Chelsea Flower Show.

If you visit the Blue Boar during the summer months, you will be able to enjoy the lovely little rose garden which Robert Mattock designed and planted a couple of years ago. And if you have time to walk round Longworth after enjoying the walk Pythius and I always take to the Thames Path, you will still see several of those old roses propagated here many years ago, still lingering on some of the old cottage walls. Many are still in full bloom during October.

The Walk

This walk is easy, providing you ignore several way signs and keep going straight down Tucks Lane which stands to the right, if you have your back to the pub. We walked a mile each way, but once you reach the Thames Path, you can extend the walk in either direction if you wish, and walk for as long as you like.

Having passed Princes Farm on the left, which was once a rose nursery, ignore the footpath sign on your left and keep going down the tarmac lane which winds down hill. You will then come to a T-junction and notice a footpath sign on the right. Ignore this sign, turn left and having walked about 10 yards, turn onto a grassy track, where a waymarker indicates that the Thames Path is a quarter of a mile away.

This track is quite wide when you begin walking it, but as you ascend Harrowdown Hill it becomes quite narrow. Not so narrow you can't walk comfortably, just narrower. Having reached the top of the hill, stop for a moment and enjoy the view of the Thames Valley to the north, which is visible when there are gaps in the hedge.

You will eventually come to a point where you discover yourself meeting two fields separated by a hedgerow. Keep the hedgerow to your left and continue walking to the bottom of the field where you will find what is best described as a human sized rabbit hole in the hedgerow. We almost went straight past this little path the first time we walked the field. It is in the far corner and well hidden – so keep your eyes peeled.

Pythius says:

I have been visiting this pub for years, because it is one of Helen's favourites. She says she has been visiting it since the present owner saved it from dereliction in the late 1970s, and that apart from the recent extensions, it hasn't changed a scrap.

As that is a long, long time ago, perhaps the less said about that the better. (Women are really funny about revealing their age! I don't know why, I have no fear about telling everyone that I am now ten years old.)

When visiting this pub I often try to settle myself beside the blazing log-fire, but never manage to stay there for long – it's far too hot, even for a Border collie who is used to sitting beside the fire in Helen's cottage.

The walk is fine, perhaps a little bit tedious as we make our way down the tarmac road. However very little traffic travels this way, only the occasional farmer transporting livestock, so Helen usually lets me off my lead so that I can walk free.

Once we get to the green lane, I have great fun, as there are some amazing foxy smells to be sniffed along the way. Loads of birdsong too. I like birdsong.

Forgive me for showing off a little by admitting that it is usually my nose that seeks out that little entrance in the corner of the field that leads to the River. Helen and Auntie Liz often walk right past by mistake. I know it's there because I can smell the river, and there is nothing I like better than a river.

Unfortunately the riverbanks in this area are rather deep, but I usually manage to find a place where I can jump in and splash about a bit when we finally get there.

Cows are often using the first field by the river, but if you take the right hand footpath towards Newbridge, you can enjoy the freedom that a river provides in true doggie style without fear of bovine intrusion.

When we have finished this walk, the girls often take me for a gentle amble around the village to seek out the old roses that can still be found there.

Having discovered this gap, you will descend through a small wooded path, which soon leads to a little stone bridge and a lovely wooden kissing gate. At this point you have reached the River Thames and the Thames Path.

To your right you will notice a superb wooden waymarker with the acorn sign that indicates you are on the Thames Path. Turn right and you will eventually come to the A415, and Newbridge, the six-arched bridge which dates back to the 13th century, where two fierce skir-

mishes were fought during the English Civil War. The Maybush Inn stands on the left and the Rose Revived Inn on the left. At the time of writing dogs were welcomed at the Maybush, but only outside on the patio at the Rose Revived.

We usually just walk to the Thames, and having let Pythius run around in the first field, gently amble back again.

The only thing you may have to watch out for once you've reached the Thames is cattle. On our last visit there were loads of moist cow-pats in this field, which suggests it is often occupied with bovine beasts.

History

Richard Doddridge Blackmore, who wrote the classic novel *Lorna Doone*, was born at the Longworth Rectory in 1825. His novel was published in 1869 and has been in print ever since.

Northmoor
The Red Lion

Only when you notice the church and the Red Lion do you realise you are in the village of Northmoor as many of the houses randomly scattered along the road are separated from each other by fields and large gardens. It's off the A415 a few miles south-east of Witney.

There used to be two pubs here, the Dun Cow, which was run by the same family for more than 100 years, and the Red Lion, which is a typical village pub.

Visiting the Dun Cow was rather like walking into someone's sitting room. The beer was dispensed straight from the barrel and heaven help anyone who didn't behave. They would be banned immediately by the formidable licensee who was rightly proud of the atmosphere this quaint little pub generated. Sadly it has now been converted into a private dwelling and only the Red Lion remains. But that's OK, the Red Lion is a great country pub which dates back to 17th century and has more beams than you can count – open fireplaces too. In fact it offers everything you would expect of a little pub which stands close to a 13th century church and serves a farming community that enjoy a well kept beer and a homely meal.

Pythius says

I used to have to wait in the car while Helen and Auntie Liz went in for lunch at The Red Lion. Now I am allowed to place my paws under the table, which is great, particularly as the resident dog seems to accept visiting canines.

I didn't get offered any water, but lots of the local farmers who called in for a lunchtime drink came over and spoke to me.

There are loads of sheep in this area, so they all seemed to like the fact I was a Border collie. One nice farmer called Glenville even spent time telling Helen which walk I would like best when she and Auntie Liz finished their lunch. We called into his farm after the walk to buy some new-laid free range eggs which was great as he keeps cows, ponies, pussy cats and geese as well as hens. Gosh what fun I would have if Helen lived on a farm like that – but she doesn't so I have to get my kicks from farms like Glenville's instead.

We did, however, have a great walk through five adjoining fields to the River Thames. It proved a really great romp, though I could see from the various juicy cow pats and sheep droppings in the fields we walked through that this walk is not always as free of livestock as it was on the day we made our way to the river.

Sunday lunches are so popular you have to book a table well in advance. It's far quieter during the week, which may be why it not only attracts locals, but residents from nearby villages who enjoy home cooked food served with a generous assortment of garden vegetables that have been harvested locally.

The previous licensee, who built the pub up to what it is today, did not permit dogs to come into the bar, but he retired in 2008 and new licensees are carrying on where he left off. To encourage walkers to use the pub, dogs are now allowed in too, providing the resident black Labrador approves of them. This means Pythius does not have to sit in the car if we call in for lunch now.

The Walk

The village is situated in the Upper Thames Valley that is designated an Enviornmentally Sensitive Conservation Area.

As there's an abundance of public footpaths and bridleways here, it attracts both walkers and cyclists, which means walking in this area on a warm sunny day is often a very social affair.

On leaving the pub, having asked permission from the landlord to leave your car in the car park, turn right and walk past the church and several houses, including a farm house that keeps a great assortment of chickens. Within a few moments you will discover a metal gate on the right hand side with a red notice saying PRIVATE FISHING.

There is a small stile besides this gate and a waymarker pointing to the river. As the stile is not particularly dog-friendly you may prefer to open the gate and enter that way, taking care to close it tightly again, because you may encounter livestock in the five fields you are about to enter. There's really no need for further instructions, as all you have to do now is follow the path that takes you from one open-plan field to the next until you reach the Thames. If you keep to the well-walked path on approaching the river, you will discover a glorious little bay where the dog can have a great time paddling freely amongst the reeds.

Should you wish you can extend your walk along the Thames Path, to Northmoor Lock if you turn left or Bablock Hythe and The Ferry Inn if you turn right. But we simply relaxed by the river then turned and went back the way we had come, which took about a hour, perhaps just a little bit more because we ambled, stopping now and again to admire the many wild flowers and butterflies that were there in abundance.

We spent a few moments visiting the Church of St Denys on the way back too. There has been a church, or perhaps a chapel of ease, on this site since the 12th century. With its minstrel gallery and 15th century tower, it's certainly worth a visit before returning to your car. The alter rails are particularly interesting and certainly worth a second look, as they are Laudian and have recently been restored to their original 17th century colour.

History

Bounded by the River Windrush to the west, the Thames to the south and east and gravel lakes to the north, Northmoor is a very watery area, which was once prone to excessive flooding during wet periods because it lies so low.

Thanks to a system of ditches dug by prisoners of war during the second world war, flooding is not such a big problem now, though many of the fields abutting the Thames are often waterlogged during exceptionally wet periods.

Oxford (Botley)
Michael at The George

Parking right next to The George, Botley Road, Oxford is difficult, but that's OK as this pub stands almost directly opposite the Seacourt park and ride, which is just a mile from the centre of Oxford and offers free all-day parking. Once parked, cross the road and you are there.

The George has had a chequered life, but it changed hands recently and is now offering a superb lunch menu at a reasonable price and great beer.

It's difficult to determine the exact age of the pub. It looks as if it has been built over several periods, the conservatory restaurant that looks out over the little Seacourt Stream probably being added last.

Its décor is difficult to describe too, for it is certainly not olde worlde, it's not stylishly modern either, though it looks far smarter now than it used to. Let's call it a smart city pub with a pubby bar area, which is friendly but unpretentious. Dining takes place in the conservatory, though if like us you arrive with a canine friend, you can enjoy lunch in the bar area.

As it stands close to several business parks and a busy little shopping centre, this pub now attracts a considerable number of people looking for a tasty, reasonably priced lunch.

Although I will always think of it as The George, since master-

caterer George Sadones took over it's now named Michael at the George. He describes his menu as traditional French cuisine with no fusion or confusion. I just describe it as tasty.

Pythius was not offered water when he arrived in the bar area where dogs are allowed, and was rather miffed about that, but all was forgiven when a bowl of ice-cold water was presented on request.

I was there to discuss gardening with my friend Anne who is planning to promote the use of locally produced herbs once she has finished her studies at horticulture college. Pythius was very patient while we talked herbs, sipped our glasses of Old Speckled Hen, and munched our way through a two-course lunch. But once he saw me paying the bill, he was up and ready for his walk.

The Walk

This walk couldn't be easier. Once you have left the pub turn right towards Oxford, walk about ten yards and you will discover a grassy lane running beside the Seacourt Stream. On the gate at the entrance is a notice announcing that you are about to enter the Seacourt Nature Park. You can let the dog off the lead immediately and simply relax

and enjoy the strange experience of walking out of a busy area clogged with cars and straight into deep countryside, complete with wild flowers and birdsong.

One of the remarkable things about this walk is that large DIY stores

Pythius says

Helen wasn't sure I'd be welcome at this pub when it changed hands, as the man who has taken it over puts his food first. But it seems he happily accepts canine visitors providing they remain in the bar area and don't venture into the restaurant.

I obliged by leading Helen to a table near the door and promptly settling myself down so that he could see how well trained I was.

I have noticed of late that Helen is quite happy for me to select our table and act as a guide dog, though as far as I know there is absolutely nothing wrong with her sight. I just think she likes the fellow in her life to take command now and again, and I am quite happy to do that. After all, if I were a working Border collie rather than a companion dog, I would be herding sheep which calls for similar skills – but don't tell her I said that!

The walk is fantastic. Within seconds of leaving the pub Helen removes my lead and allows me to run wherever I like as long as I steer clear of the horses and the electric fence. I really love this place and, like Helen, find it difficult to accept that lush green pastures can sit so close to a main road leading into Oxford. We come here often with Auntie Liz. My only complaint is that the stream is not much to talk about, too many reeds and weeds and not enough water.

and industrial buildings are intermittently visible through gaps in the hedgerow, but this doesn't spoil the walk. There is also a spot where you can view Oxford's dreaming spires (well, some of them). The large electricity pylons that cross the main field and vanish into the far distance are another sign that this green lung that you are exploring stands close to an industrial side of the city. Yes, it's all very strange.

We ignored a grass lane leading off to the left and kept walking, arriving at a field fenced off with electric ribbons, as two magnificent horses are housed there. Worry not about this, as standing beside the fence you will find a stile for humans and a dog shaped hole for dogs to get through. Someone has written the word Dogs on the board above this hole, and drawn an arrow to let the dogs know where they have to go. On similar stiles that you will undoubtedly encounter along the way, you may be amused to notice that someone else has written 'Dogs & Gnomes' above the arrow.

The field you have entered is large and abuts the leafy lane that runs from an industrial estate to Hinksey. This is now called Willow Walk and is a medieval causeway for foot traffic only which was first opened up as a public path in 1923.

There are metal kissing gates on all four sides of the field, allowing you to join Willow Walk or other fields along the way. This means that people and their dogs are constantly weaving their way in and out of the field from all corners and occasionally entering Willow Walk.

We followed a well-worn path right across the field and alongside the Seacourt Stream towards Willow Walk. Having made our way through a metal kissing gate we turned left, and walked this attractive little lane until we arrived at the point where a large pylon stands proud and next to another kissing gate on the left.

This took us back into the field we'd first entered. Had we gone further, we would have crossed a small bridge and passed a playing field before arriving at the industrial estate and *The Oxford Times* office.

If you want a longer walk, you will notice another kissing gate on the right just before the pylon. This leads to a little lane, which in turn leads to the water meadows we so enjoy walking when we call at The Fishes in North Hinksey, further down the road. The Fishes is one of Pythius's favourite pubs, so we often walk the water meadows, but usually begin that walk by turning left when we leave The Fishes, taking the first stile on the left a little further along the road.

By entering the water meadows down that little lane you can extend your walk for miles if you wish. Pythius loves going that way. However, on the day we visited the George we ambled for about a mile across fields that ran parallel with the Botley Road.

History

Despite the fact that the Seacourt Stream is not an important river now, it actually formed the border between Mercia and Wessex in Anglo-Saxon times. Later it acted as part of the boundary between Berkshire and Oxfordshire until the boundary changed in 1974, when parts of Berkshire were moved into Oxfordshire.

Oxford (Walton Manor) The Anchor Inn

The Anchor Inn, Hayfield Road, in North Oxford is a relatively new pub, built in 1937, yet because it has retained its splendid Art Deco interior it oozes with as much atmosphere as an ancient tavern. It really is a splendid pub – one of my favourites, actually.

There's a small car park at the rear but as it is often full during busy periods, I usually park the car at nearby Wolvercote and walk a mile along the canal bank to get there.

This is the pub that has played host to Oxford's alternative May Morning ceremony, ever since the event was first organised by sculptor Michael Black in 1989. In the early 1970s, Michael carved the 13 new heads which adorn the columns outside the Sheldonian Theatre, Oxford, and who later carved a further four for the Museum of the History of Science next door. As a resident of North Oxford, he devised a suitable setting for the alternative May Morning ceremony by building a 20 foot high replica of Magdalen Tower and a life-size glass fibre ox which is pushed over the little bridge in Aristotle Lane by a band of Morris Men. Early-bird revellers attending at 6 a.m., wearing fancy hats and May blossom in their hair, join in singing some really silly songs on the bridge, then tip into the Anchor Inn to enjoy steaming hot bacon butties and several glasses of real ale, while being serenaded by the Eynsham Morris. It's far more fun than joining the crowds on Magdalen Bridge in the centre of Oxford.

Dogs are certainly welcome at the Anchor Inn, but are asked to sit in the small bar to the left on entering the pub, as the main bar is now doubling as a very popular restaurant run by a couple with vision who have devised a simply scrumptious menu.

The food is not cheap here, but where possible it is locally sourced and everything is cooked to order from scratch. Their beef and ale pie is particularly good and comes with crunchy hand-cut chips which are absolutely delicious.

As it's a Wadworth pub, Henry's Original IPA and Bishop's Tipple were on tap the day we called, as well as Young's Special. All the beers are well kept and definitely served with a smile as this is one of those happy pubs where the beer is taken as seriously as the food. Despite upgrading the menu, the current licensees have managed to retain their local beer trade and the convivial atmosphere for which this pub has always been known.

The Walk

It's worth saying that during the winter months this can turn into a very wet and muddy walk, so waterproof boots are necessary.

If you do as we did on our last trip to the Anchor Inn, you will need to take the first turning left on driving into Wolvercote from the A40 roundabout. This will takes you past the Village Hall on the left and Wolvercote Green on the right towards the Plough Inn, where unfortunately dogs are not allowed. Once you reach the Plough it is a matter of finding a space to park your car along the street before entering Wolvercote Green. Cross a small bridge directly opposite the pub, and steps on the left will take you down the canal path. Turn towards Oxford and enjoy a leisurely walk along the towpath for about a mile, passing narrow boats, swans and a housing development.

On arriving at bridge number 239a (all canal bridges are numbered), take the path up the slope and over the red brick bridge, turning right into Hayfield Road. Here you will be entering the suburb of Walton Manor, and passing some of the attractive two-up and two-down Victorian redbrick terraced houses, originally built for workers of

Lucy's Iron Works, which are now highly prized by students, academics and those who work in the City.

The Anchor Inn stands on the corner where Hayfield Road meets Polstead Road. Having stopped at the pub for refreshments, cross the road and enter Aristotle Lane, which is directly opposite the pub. Walk over the bridge, passing a new housing development on your right, until the point where the road sweeps to the right into Navigation Way and to a primary school. Just where the road begins to turn you will notice a small lane flanked by a redbrick wall. Take this lane, turning left when the lane forks, and continue over a long bridge covered with graffiti. You are now in Port Meadow, one of Oxford's most popular green lungs.

To return to Wolvercote you have to bear right and head for the houses in the far distance. How you get to Wolvercote at this point is really up to you, though the weather might well determine which path you follow, as the meadow frequently floods during the winter months.

The last time Auntie Liz and I took Pythius this way, we turned right, skirting the floods and then, having turned a corner, entered the gate leading to Burgess Field nature reserve, which provides the walker with 35 acres of wild open space and many paths to choose from. This area, which stands on the eastern side of Port Meadow, used to be a refuge tip. It was planted up twenty years ago. Due to the various types of topsoil used to cap the tip, a rich variety of wild flowers grows here. You will find some remarkable birds too, including skylarks that fill the air with their song during the summer months. It really is a glorious place to walk. BUT, and yes there is a but, if you don't follow the main path adjacent to Port Meadow, you will find some of the paths are circular and may not realise this until you end up at the place where you first started.

We eventually discovered a metal kissing gate on the left-hand side which took us back to Port Meadow and Wolvercote.

Pythius says

Well I must admit that the walk along the canal is a bit restrictive for a dog like me who likes to run in circles. But knowing that I was heading toward the Anchor Inn where I could sit beside the fire while Helen and Auntie Liz ate their lunch, and would then have a run through Port Meadow – I coped well enough. If I am honest I rather enjoyed it actually, as there are many interesting sights to see and doggie smells in abundance.

Once we reached Port Meadow I was in doggie heaven as the floods covered a substantial part of the meadow. This enabled me to run and run and run, splashing through the floods with no concern about getting out of my depth. Things did change when we got to Burgess Field as there are no floods there, just mud now and again and lots of green pathways leading all over the place.

At first Auntie Liz, Helen and I really enjoyed ourselves, walking down different pathways at whim, but then came a bit of a disaster (which as usual Helen hasn't described in depth, because she is probably a little embarrassed). After walking for some considerable time they suddenly realised they were lost and had no idea how to get back into Port Meadow. At first they laughed nervously and kept throwing my ball – but there came a time when Helen started to get uptight and in a bit of a panic – she had an important appointment that evening and had to be home by 4 pm.

It was Auntie Liz who came to the rescue (she hadn't spent all those years as an Army nurse for nothing). She pointed out the kissing gate that would take us to Port Meadow. Helen shook her head: "No", she said. "It leads straight into a stream and the floods; we will never get over them."

Auntie Liz ignored her protests, pointed out that we could indeed wade over as someone had left a plank of wood in the stream. I won't go into details, but those who know of Helen's protective feelings towards that beloved camera of hers and her fear of falling into the water will be aware of her concern. Gosh, there are times when she is a real wimp.

I think it was her need to get home in time for that special appointment that spurred her on. Stoically, Auntie Liz led the way regardless of the fact that her boots were covered with water, while I waded in the stream beside them. Within minutes we had reached the other side and joined up with a well-worn path that led them the meadow back to Wolvercote. As they walked towards the meadow car park, their boots oozed water and they were distinctly uncomfortable! I just wonder why she didn't admit that when discussing the walk?

By the way, the other thing Helen has not explained is that if you get back to Port Meadow, you will probably land up at the Wolvercote car park, which means you have another quarter of a mile to walk. On reaching the car park you have to turn right through the village, and on along the Godstow Road, over the railway bridge and on until you reach Wolvercote Green.

Because we got lost several times whilst walking Burgess Field, our walk was extended somewhat. I guess we walked at least four miles in total. Nevertheless, it was a glorious walk as we were constantly stimulated by the wide assortment of views, bird song and unusual plants. Pythius had the most amazing time too rushing in and out of the floodwaters and running around Burgess Field. We keep him under control in this area when ground-nesting birds are using the space.

History

Port Meadow (originally known as Portmaneit or Burgess Island) dates back to the tenth century and the days of King Alfred who gave the meadow to the Freemen of Oxford in return for fighting the Danish invaders.

Because the meadow has never been ploughed it contains well preserved archaeological remains from the Iron Age.

During the English Civil War, when Charles I was using Oxford as his headquarters, he billeted his forces on Port Meadow.

On the night of June 3 1644 he left Oxford, marching his troops through the area now named Jericho and on to Aristotle Lane, before crossing the river into Port Meadow from where he headed for the West Country.

Quenington
The Keeper's Arms

It's worth visiting Quenington, if only for the glorious drive through the Cotswolds that you need to make to get there. The scenery as we turned off the A40 onto the B4425 towards Bibury and then on to Quenington is spectacular, particularly in October when the many mature trees in this area don their autumn colours. This is the moment when nature uses a rich palette of fire, russet and gold to paint the Cotswold's rolling landscapes. The result is a series of breathtaking views unique to the area. Quenington stands close to the River Coln and is on the Fosse Way.

The Keeper's Arms, Church Street, stands on the road that runs through the eastern side of the village green and down towards the little 12th century church, with its spectacular carvings over the south and north doors.

This pub is thought to be at least 300 years old, beginning life as two small gamekeeper's cottages, but no one could give me an exact date, though we were told it was once named The Pack Horse.

Whilst it does have a small car park at the back, it is just as easy to park in the road outside the pub. While we were there we counted only half a dozen cars using this road, so parking really isn't a problem.

Apparently this glorious little Cotswold village seldom attracts cars as visitors tend to arrive on foot, having walked from nearby Bibury or Coln St Aldwyns.

This pub is reputed to be haunted by a ghost called Fred, who is quite friendly providing he likes you. He must have liked us, for Pythius's nose didn't twitch once while we were there and we certainly weren't conscious of a ghostly presence.

The bar area is delightful, small, friendly and everything we had hoped for, including gnarled beams, brass and copper ware and a good assortment of atmospheric pictures of the area. Pythius was made to feel very welcome, there was absolutely no problem about him joining us.

While we were there a gorgeous black Labrador led his owner to the bar. Once he was settled the Lab turned his attention to Pythius. I am sure they smiled knowingly at each other momentarily as the Lab settled down beside his master. Dogs who visit pubs frequently seem to understand the score, which includes guiding their masters to the bar and then settling down while they enjoy a pint or two, because when a glass is finally emptied, a walk normally follows.

There are two main areas in this pub – the Keeper's Bar and the Poacher's Bar and a small cosy dining area. The draught beer on tap included Wickwar's Cotswold Way, a well balanced, rich amber beer with a terrific hoppy finish. The perfect beer if walking the Cotswolds – well, we certainly enjoyed it. Pythius made do with the water that was placed outside the front door for visiting canines.

The food is well prepared, reasonably priced and nicely served and the choice includes the usual pub specials one would expect, along with a few fancy dishes such as crispy duck salad. It's worth remembering that meals are not served Sunday evenings or Monday and Tuesday.

The first walk

As Quenington features in the Doomsday Book and was once the home of the Knights Hospitallers, it is steeped in history.

By turning left after leaving the pub and walking a few hundred yards down Church Street you can view a 13th century gatehouse, the only surviving building from a preceptory estate of the Knights (see photo on p115).

Pythius says

Oh dear, there are times when Auntie Liz and Helen really do get in a muddle. I am sure that they get that big paper map of theirs upside down sometimes, which might account for why we didn't find the river walk the first time round.

Also – Helen does not always tell the full story, or simply leaves things out – let me explain. When they went over the second stone stile during the first walk, having climbed a stone staircase to get there, there was no sign of any kind stating what might or might not be in the field.

They climbed the stile with confidence, stood for simply ages getting all poetic about the scenery when they had reached the high point of the field, and then chattered away about what a find this was as we made our way to the stile leading to Quenington's Mawley Road.

What Helen has failed to explain is that on reaching the end of the walk we encountered a big yellow sign on the wall by the stile saying Bull in Field. Actually, I don't think there was a bull in the field that day. There was certainly no evidence of squashy wet bull pats, but there could have been and then we would all have been in trouble!

It was quite amusing as they went silent on reading the sign, in fact I didn't get a single word out of them until we reached Church Road. So, the reason why Helen has included a second walk that starts at the bridge that leads to Coln St Aldwyns may be as much to do with the bull field as the fact they wanted to give me a river walk.

Unfortunately, when we did attempt the river walk (which was the following week, and not the same day as they ran out of time after walk one) that was full of hazards too.

I admit feeling rather sorry for them, as they were so full of it when they made the second journey to Quenington. All those promises they made about

the river and everything – none of which came to much because of the sign on the gate and the little baby calves we discovered in the second field.

I was kept on a lead throughout, apart from one little field, which appeared empty. Poor things, they were so disappointed, and if I am really honest so was I.

Whilst walking this way, it is worth turning the corner and visiting the church of St Swithin just a few yards away. It's here you will discover what must be the tidiest churchyard in the Cotswolds, as all grave stones have been placed along the walls to provide a large expanse of neatly groomed lawn. It is indeed a tranquil place.

Turn and walk back towards the pub after viewing the church, taking Victoria Road, which is the first on the right. It's worth walking this way just to view the many glorious old houses that line the road. Every time the road turns a little there are more and more picturesque homes built from the glorious honey-coloured Cotswold stone.

When the houses peter out, you will find two stone stiles either side of the road. Take the stile on the right and you are in a large meadow, which abuts the River Coln. Much to Pythius's delight, we followed the path across the meadow, then left it for the river... only to discover a sign stating STRICTLY PRIVATE FISHING – NO FOOTPATH.

Despondent, we returned back across the field to Victoria Road, climbed the stone steps to the other stile and found ourselves in another lovely meadow which, after a steep climb, provided us with a view to die for. Words can't describe it. The combination of green fields, trees touched with autumnal colours and clusters of little houses took our breath away, such that we stopped for several moments to take it all in despite the fact that Pythius was getting bored and wanted to go on.

To the left of the field is a green lane along with another stone stile that leads to Mawley Road, and another little lane that took us back to Church Street and the pub.

We had taken so long ambling along this route that we had left no time to take the river walk to Bibury as we'd intended. Because this area was so beautiful, we decided to return and take that walk another day, which is why I've listed two walks beginning at The Keeper's Arms. This means if you want a gentle amble, a historic gatehouse, a Norman church and some amazing views of the Coln valley, enjoy the walk I've just described.

If you want to take a longer walk, the next one is what you want, providing you are prepared to walk through fields full of livestock during the spring and summer period.

The second walk

Turning left on leaving the pub you have a road walk for at least half a mile as you keep bearing right past the village green towards Coln St Aldwyns.

You soon reach a stone bridge crossing the River Coln. Just before the bridge you will discover a bridle path sign, half covered with foliage. It points to a path that requires you to walk through a white gate and past a little stone house through what appears to be someone's garden until you get to a wooden gate. It's at this point that we were slightly disappointed, as the sign on the gate reads: PLEASE KEEP TO THE FOOTPATH, AND KEEP AWAY FROM THE RIVERBANK. NO PADDLING. NO PICNICS.

We could have lived with that, we even coped with the sheep in the first field, but were somewhat dismayed to discover cows with young calves in the next field.

If you are prepared to cope with these hazards, then walk on and enjoy the undulating landscape, which is quite breathtaking.

The well-worn footpath that will take you to Bibury skirts the river

most of the way, but be assured the views are outstanding.

Having passed through semi-wooded areas and many gates bearing waymarks you will arrive at a track above the valley. When you reach Court Farm and its stone-built farmhouse on the right, another waymarker guides you round a mill, granary and dovecote, then across the River Coln at Bibury Court Hotel. You can now either retrace your footsteps at this point or explore Bibury first.

This is quite a long walk, possibly three miles each way – but be assured, if you have the energy and your dog is good with livestock if kept on a lead, it is well worth the effort.

History

The manor of Quenington was given to the Hospitallers by Agness de Lucy and her daughter Sibila and a preceptory was established there c1193. The preceptory was dissolved in 1540. The impressive gateway is the only remnant that survives.

The Knights Hospitallers were created from a religious brotherhood who cared for sick pilgrims in a hospital in Jerusalem, following the first Crusade in 1100. The community at Quenington consisted of the preceptor, two other knights, a chaplain, three clerks and several servants.

Southrop
The Swan

Southrop lies three miles north-east of Fairford. It is a particularly attractive little Cotswold village which borders the watermeadows of the River Leach, which form its eastern boundary. To the west, the scarp slope of the Cotswolds provides steep hillsides and dramatic views. To the east is a gently sloping, undulating landscape, which is what we explored when visiting the village.

Unfortunately we misjudged the weather forecast completely when Uncle John and I set out with Pythius to take the four mile circular walk from Southrop to Eastleach and back. The man on the radio suggested it would be warm – but it turned out to be one of the few very hot days of summer.

As a consequence we were totally exhausted by the time we arrived at the Swan Inn. We were desperately thirsty too.

Imagine, therefore how wonderful it was to arrive at this glorious ivy-clad 17th century inn on Southrop's village green and discover that the young barman spotted our plight immediately.

"You will be wanting some water first?" he said, as he reached for a dog bowl that was instantly filled with cool water. Having placed this on the floor beside Pythius, he then poured us both a glass of ice cold water too, then stood back and waited for us to recover from the heat. Gosh, we were impressed. That was service with a capital S.

This inn is run by Sebastian and Lana Snow. As Sebastian is a protégé of the celebrity chef Antony Worrall Thompson and the couple ran their acclaimed West London restaurant Snows on the Green from the early nineties, they obviously know all about good service and good food, which is why we were made so welcome.

This is one of those country inns that is light and airy in the summer, and cosy in the winter months when the many log fires are burning brightly. The décor is stylish and rustic and the menu amazing, as it not only provides great choice for those seeking gourmet food, but it caters for people like Uncle John and me who were only looking for basic refreshments – a sandwich or reasonably priced baguette.

Actually the portions we were served proved so generous it took us some time to finish our lunch, which bore out my theory that walkers

should not be afraid of using a stylish pub like this. Our food was simply scrumptious and cost no more than we would have paid elsewhere. The beer's good too.

The Walk

This is a circular walk which covers about four miles and includes a river walk, and takes in another lovely dog-friendly Cotswold pub which stands at the half way point, where you can stop for a break.

Having left our car outside the pub, we turned left past the school and Pear Tree Cottage where a footpath sign is fixed to the cottage wall. This takes you down a narrow lane to a stone stile.

This stile is quite high. Pythius managed it in one leap, but some dogs might find it difficult. Once over the stile you will find yourself on a green path which eventually opens up into a large field. You must aim to turn right at this point, follow the edge of the field to the corner, where there is an opening just a few yards further on that leads to an ancient stone bridge over the river Leach. There were large somnolent cows in this field, sheltering in the shade of trees along the path, the day we took this walk, so we had to make a big sweep past them. It was so hot they didn't move or respond to our presence.

On reaching the river, turn immediately left and keeping the river on your left follow a really picturesque little path, which emerges into a country road. It's advisable to put the dog on the lead at this point and

> ## Pythius Says
>
> I have been to Northleach before and rather like the river Leach as the water is crisp, fragrant and cool. There's a smashing little dog-friendly pub there, where I am always welcome and the locals talk to me. But I hadn't visited Southrop before, so this walk had the makings of a great day out discovering new tracks and smells and splashing about in another part of this delightful river.
>
> I guess it would have been really fantastic if there had been water all the way there and back, but there wasn't. We met the river for a short part of the walk and I certainly enjoyed that, but that wasn't enough for what seemed the hottest day of the year.
>
> Although Helen always packs a bottle of water and my doggie bowl in her rucksack if we are doing a long walk on a hot summer's day, the water she was carrying this time became so warm, it hardly touched the spot. All I can say is thank goodness for that lovely young man at the Swan, who on spotting my plight, came to my aid immediately. Gosh I was grateful to him. I certainly liked that pub and the joy of being able to curl up on a cool floor and relax as Helen and Uncle John munched away on a couple of fat baguettes. They certainly seemed to enjoy the food they were served and appeared to like their beers too. Actually, I am sure if Uncle John had not been driving, he would have ordered another one – yes he was that thirsty.

turn right for about 25 yards, entering a field on your left onto a well-walked path. We walked this way, went through a wheat field, then a field full of clover and then another wheat field before the path finally emerges onto a narrow country lane, which if you turn left, leads towards the village of Eastleach, which lies in the valley below.

The fields are large, and with the sun blazing down, we began to fear its heat, so our progress was not rapid.

At this point it is worth explaining that Eastleach comprises two villages, Eastleach Martin and Eastleach Turville, which are only separated by the River Leach. They both boast attractive churches that are but a stone's throw from each other.

You will find the Victoria Inn at the far end of Eastleach Turville, raised slightly from the road. You reach it by walking past the village war memorial on your right, then walking straight ahead and uphill. Dogs are always welcomed here and so are walkers. The food is home cooked and the assortment of Arkell's beers on tap would gladden the heart of anyone who enjoys real ale.

After resting and enjoying the unspoiled beauty of this delightful little village that looks as if it has emerged effortlessly out of the ground on which it stands, return to Southrop. Before leaving The Victoria take a moment to admire the view that has not changed for centuries. You will feel that time has stood still as the rural history of this glorious little place envelopes you.

Now take the road to Eastleach, the second of two roads that passes in front of the pub. Turn left walking downhill until you come to a footpath leading to an ancient stone clapper bridge crossing the Leach to St Michael and St Martin's church, which is certainly worth a visit, even though it is no longer used for regular services. During the spring this spot is noted for its fabulous display of daffodils.

Having visited the church, walk back a little way up the hill and look for Verderers Cottage and turn right, then after 30 yards (just before Bourne Cottage) turn right again, and then left almost immediately. At this point you will observe a waymarker that sets you on the footpath home.

As you cross this field, you will discover a line of trees and may notice some very handsome horses grazing here, so keep an eye on your dog, putting him on a lead if necessary.

Keep the trees to your left and walk on until the path divides, taking the right hand turn past a farmhouse. You will encounter a driveway that links with the lone farmhouse, cross this and follow a well worn path over a wooden stile, and a couple more fields. The last field is the one you first entered. You can now return the way you came or bear right towards the end of the field where you will discover a gate which takes you back to the Swan if you turn left.

History

One of the fascinating things about this area is the fact that the curate of the church of St Michael and St Martin, Eastleach Martin, during the early 19th century was John Keble, a leader of the Oxford Movement in the Church of England, in whose memory Keble College, Oxford was founded. He was a popular figure in the twin villages, founding a Sunday School and becoming firm friends with the locals. The picturesque clapper bridge between the two villages is named after him.

St Michael and St Martin is now cared for by The Churches Conservation Trust.

Stoke Row
The Cherry Tree Inn

The red-bricked Cherry Tree Inn stands just a little way back from the main road that runs through the south Oxfordshire village of Stoke Row. Not only is this area the highest point of the southern Chiltern hills, it is situated in a region of outstanding natural beauty. It is equidistant from Wallingford, Reading and Henley and is close to the Ridgeway, the Thames Path and the Thames Valley Cycle Routes.

This delightful Brakspear pub was originally three flint cottages dating back to the 1700s. It has been a pub for more than 200 years. Although it was given a major re-fit several years ago, it retains its polished flagstone floors, beamed ceilings and open fireplaces. As it stands close to a heavily wooded area, there is no shortage of fuel to keep the fires blazing during the winter months.

Pythius is allowed in the small bar area by the entrance and is always treated cordially, water being available on request.

It's the staff's laid-back approach that generates this pub's relaxed and comfortable atmosphere. The lively knot of locals who are usually clustered round the bar give it an extra edge on other pubs in the area which are often devoid of local trade. Naturally Pythius ends up making friends with them before he leaves.

The food philosophy here is simple – the chef goes for fresh local ingredients were possible, which are presented perfectly, but without unnecessary trimmings. The menu features a wide choice of classic

European dishes served with a modern twist, and several imaginative, reasonably priced bar snacks including dishes of fried whitebait, pots of prawns and mussels cooked with chilli. We often go for the

traditional roast, when visiting on a Sunday, which tastes absolutely fantastic.

As it's a Brakspear pub, we usually choose Brakspear's Oxford Gold to go with it and when we arrive after a long walk, as it is particularly refreshing.

Food is available throughout the week, but the pub closes at 5pm on Sunday evenings to give the staff a break.

The Walk

No walk through Stoke Row would be complete without first paying homage to the Maharajah's Well. It's hard to imagine that a place like Stoke Row was once so short of water that a Maharajah from India presented the village with a well in the 19th century – but that's what happened. You will discover the newly painted well, with its gold elephant and ornate metal canopy, just before you reach the pub if you are travelling from the north. Beside the well you will notice a charming little cottage that looks rather like a honey pot, which was also part of the Maharajah's charitable gift and built for the keeper of the well.

Between the cottage and the well you will discover one of the best-kept footpaths ever. Every hedge is trimmed within an inch of its life, not a single leaf appears out of place. Take this path, which leads to Cox's Lane, a small tarmac road, turning left and walking straight ahead when you reach it. Keep walking past several houses on the left and on a little way until the tarmac turns to a dirt track and you can see farm buildings on the right.

At this point it becomes difficult as you have three paths to choose from and something (a highsided farm vehicle perhaps?) has damaged the waymarker which is rather tangled and appears to be pointing to the farm entrance. Ignore the sign and the lanes leading to the farm and keep straight ahead, taking what soon becomes a very muddy lane, that eventually widens out as you progress.

After less than a quarter of a mile, you will need to look for a stile on the right hand side. We missed this the first time, and had to double back, only spotting it because Pythius was already standing there waiting for us to lift the wire and help him through. Gosh, he is just too clever at times. This leads to a very large field, and eventually another stile and another field. Keep walking straight over both fields, keeping the fence on your left.

The next stile at the end of the second field may well prove a

Pythius Says

Yes, this pub gets ten marks out of ten from me. I love it here, everyone is so pleased to see me when we visit and the wood fires are so snuggly and warm. Must admit it is a tiny bit posh, but that's to be expected in any area close to Henley. I don't mind at all because horsey people and gentlemen farmers seem to like border collies.

As for the walk, well I loved it. All that mud to roll in down the first lane. Then in the autumn there are the rustling leaves that make a lovely crackling noise when you leap on them – great fun.

What did cause a bit of a blip was the wretched moment Uncle John consulted the map and began to shake his head. He knew we had gone too far, and so did I actually. But of course when I pointed out the stile on first passing it, they didn't take any notice. So – when we headed back I galloped down the lane until I reached the stile and simply waited for them to catch me up. Helen thought I was being naughty. I guess she would have probably told me off had she not noticed I was standing beside the stile they had been looking for. The

trouble with Helen, as I have probably remarked before, is that she has her head in the clouds and never looks left and right, whereas I am closer to the ground and can see the things she fails to spot. I have to admit they did congratulate me when they discovered I was far cleverer than them.

I won't say much about the stile that was covered with wire. How humiliating that was – fancy me having to be lifted over a stile! Unfortunately, if we were to continue the walk there was no alternative as it really was far too high for even me to leap over as I usually do. The rest of the walk was fun, particularly when we trotted through the woods which were full of the most glorious smells. Doggie heaven actually.

problem if your dog is not able to climb stiles, or is too heavy to be lifted over. Unlike the other stiles encountered along the way, there is no dog hole, and the wire surrounding the stile has been fixed far too tightly allow a dog through.

With Uncle John standing one side and lifting Pythius over and me standing the other side we managed to solve the problem – but it wasn't easy and we got covered in mud in the process.

This stile leads to a narrow restricted byway and you have the choice of going left or right. We turned right and trotted on until it opened out into a firm tarmac road with woods on the right hand side. A quarter of a mile on you will spot a waymarker to Stoke Row (1 mile) that directs you right and through the woods. If you miss this marker, there is another a little further on. (Yes – we missed the first one!)

The path is now well marked, and fenced off from the woods in places. It's all very atmospheric at this point, particularly during the autumn, when golden leaves carpet the path and an assortment of birds over-wintering here are singing their hearts out.

When you come to an opening and field in which horses graze, look for a rather narrow path straight ahead, with a couple of houses to the left. Follow this path, even though it doesn't look very substantial, as it eventually leads to another small open space and the back of the Crooked Billet pub and Newlands Lane. Turn left, pass the pub and keep to this road, which after a short distance will bring you the centre of Stoke Row, with the Cherry Tree to your right. We took about two hours to complete this walk the first time as we failed to spot the stile and waymarker pointing right, and so walked far too far down the lane. I guess the walk is about three miles if you don't lose your way.

History

The story of the Maharajah's Well began in the middle of the 19th century when the Indian ruler, the Maharajah of Benares, met Edward Anderson Reade from Stoke Row, who went on to became the Lieutenant-Governor of the North West Provinces of India.

During their many conversations he told the Maharajah that people in his home village of Stoke Row relied on rainwater for their cooking and that pond water was often used for washing. When the pond ran dry washing was postponed until it filled again.

Because Edward Anderson Reade provided help and support to the Maharajah during the Indian Mutiny, he never forgot this kindness. To express his gratitude for this help during a difficult time, the Maharajah presented the village with the well and a cottage where the well-keeper could live. He also built a cherry orchard in the next field, which he hoped would provide the people of Stoke Row with an income.

The well, which was dug by hand, goes to a depth of 368 feet, which is more than twice the height of Nelson's Column.

Sutton Courtenay
The George and Dragon

You won't find Sutton Courtenay mentioned in old books on Oxfordshire, as it was a Berkshire village until the boundary changes of 1974. However, this delightful little village, which stands on the right hand bank of the Thames and just three miles south of Abingdon, dates back to Stone Age times.

It is not, nevertheless, an area to visit during flood alerts. Due to its close proximity to the river, dog walks are best enjoyed during dry periods.

We arrived mid-September on one of those glorious autumn days when the sun shone intermittently to light up the jumble of red slate roofs, Tudor chimneys and whitewashed thatched cottages that add much character to this village.

The George and Dragon, Church Street, which is painted in Greene King's standard yellow, trimmed with dark green, stands in the centre of the village next to the village green. This cosy 16th century pub opens at noon and we had got there at 11.45am. But that was fine, it gave us time to explore the churchyard next door, where two famous men are buried.

All Saints' Church is unusual in that it has a brick-built south porch built with money left to the poor of the parish by the 15th century Bishop Thomas Bekynton of Bath and Wells. It's a superb addition that gives this church its character, though we did find ourselves wondering if the poor of the parish would have benefited more from handouts of food and clothing rather than a church porch.

We were there to seek out the burial place of Eric Arthur Blair – known to readers of *Animal Farm* and *Nineteen Eighty Four* as George Orwell.

The note pinned to the church door instructs visitors to follow the right hand line of yew trees to the east, as his grave is behind the fourth tree. It took us a while, as there's an abundance of mature yews lining the walkways, but in the end we discovered a modest little grave, on which one white and one red rose bush flourish.

The churchyard also contains the grave of Lord Herbert Henry Asquith, Earl of Oxford, and prime minister from 1908 to 1916, whose achievements include the introduction of the old age pension. Unfortunately the church is locked so we were unable to explore further.

The George and Dragon is one of those delightful rural pubs that has not been given a make-over. The toilets are well designed and modern, but you have to go outside to find them.

It is cosy and welcoming, particularly during the winter months when the fire is lit and the locals are crowded round the bar enjoying a pint or two of real ale. There is a small restaurant here too, but most people tend to eat in the bar at lunch time.

A bowl of water is placed inside the main door for visiting canines and a large glass jar of dog biscuits sits at the far end of the bar, which indicates that dogs are welcome here. Actually they are made so welcome in the bar area that Pythius was offered a dog biscuit from the jar before the staff asked us what we would like to drink!

As it is a Greene King pub and we were visiting during the autumn, we ordered half pints of

Pythius says

The pub is great. I have never been offered a biscuit from a dog biscuit jar before – that was fantastic, particularly as I was served before Helen and Auntie Liz were asked what they would like.

What Helen has not admitted in describing the day, is that she promised me a real river walk where I could jump in and out of the water and really have a great time. She and Auntie Liz both spent some time consulting the village map outside the pub to check which path would provide a watery walk, but they got it wrong!

To get to the part of the river that dogs would like, they should have followed the first footpath sign just past The Wharf where Mr Asquith the prime minister once lived. The sign, which can be found just as the road turns to the right into Appleford Road, just before you reach The Fish, is slightly obscured by overhanging greenery. They were chatting so much as they admired the amazing old houses in Church Street, they missed this sign altogether, and assumed that the sign opposite The Fish was the right one. It wasn't.

The walk we did was fine, no real complaints, except that the riverbanks were so steep I couldn't find anywhere which allowed me to get to the water. When we reached the bridge the walk seemed to grind to a halt as we headed for dense undergrowth. Confronted with a dead end we had to turn back. Not

the best for a dog, though it was good to have a really spacious field to run around in. I liked that.

When they crossed the road and took the bridle path that passed the churchyard they kept me close to them. There was no traffic as such, but it was not an area that gave me space to play, though they seemed to enjoy circumnavigating the village and gazing at the spacious back gardens that you can't see from the main road.

We ended up back at the pub without me having a single romp in the river; nevertheless, it was a nice leisurely walk.

Conkers Bonkers, a crisp nutty brew created especially for the autumnal period.

The food menu is not fancy; we weren't expecting it to be. It's not that kind of place. This is a pub where steak pie and fish and chips are the order of the day. There's a fine selection of freshly cut sandwiches too. Although the pub has a large beer garden, we stayed in the bar and soaked up the atmosphere of this delightful hostelry.

The Walk

There is a village map erected on the village green close to the pub that highlights the houses of importance and the many footpaths in the area. It is worth consulting this before embarking on a walk.

We made for the footpath that stands opposite The Fish, another public house which can be reached from the George and Dragon in less than four minutes, by turning right out of the main door and making your way up Church Street and round the corner into Appleford Road. The footpath is clearly marked, though first you have to walk down a rather manicured area towards a wooden stile.

Once you reach the stile the dog can be let off the lead as you are entering a large meadow, with the river running to your left. The footpath marker states that this is a half mile walk along the Thames Path, but we decided it was no more than half a mile there and back. Regrettably there comes a moment when, on reaching the foot of the bridge straddling the river, the vegetation is so dense you have to turn back. Access to the bridge is not possible.

Yes, we turned back, and on reaching the main road again, put Pythius back on his lead and decided to take the bridleway across the road and alongside The Fish. This is marked All Saints' Lane and bends round the back of the village, passing the rear of the churchyard, turning right and on (eventually) to the main road.

We loved this winding lane as it offered us a chance to see the amazing array of red bricked rooftops, Tudor chimneys and spacious back-gardens of the many ancient timber-framed cottages that make up this village.

On following the path, as it winds to the right on passing the church-yard, we discovered a glorious unspoilt meadow on the left. There were no gates barring our way so we explored further. This gave Pythius a chance to run and run to his heart's delight, before being put back on his lead as we met up with the main road.

Turning right on reaching the main road we followed the tree-lined road that leads back to the village green and The George and Dragon where we had left the car.

The walk to the river and then round the village was probably not much more than a mile. But we enjoyed it. So did Pythius.

History

Archaeological finds in this area have included flint tools that date back to 6000 BC.

Written records of its history began in 688, and obviously it was mentioned in the Domesday Book of 1086. In other words, if you are looking for a picturesque village that oozes with history, and has a village green that has been the centre of the village for more than 1,000 years, Sutton Courtenay comes highly recommended.

Thrupp
The Boat

Thrupp is a pretty little hamlet a couple of miles north of the centre of Kidlington. You reach it by turning right off the A4260 which leads to Deddington and Banbury. Its main attraction is water, as it stands close to both the River Cherwell and the Oxford Canal, which on reaching Thrupp turns away from the river in a right-angle around Manor Farm in order to approach Oxford along the valley of the River Thames.

In high summer when a multitude of narrow boats are passing through Thrupp, it's a very colourful and buzzing little place, which is well worth a visit, particularly as its pub The Boat is one of those fantastic little pubs which extends a warm welcome to everyone, whatever the weather.

The pub boasts a large well-kept garden and a small restaurant, but we always head for the bar, which has an unpretentious little room adjoining it where we usually sit for lunch as Pythius is made welcome here. A bowl of cold water is always offered the moment he walks in.

As it's a Greene King pub, Abbot Ale and Old Speckled Hen are often on tap, and the food is certainly worth ordering as the current

licensee, who does all the cooking himself, believes in buying local produce whenever possible. The menu is imaginative for although it includes lots of traditional pub favourites, a few special dishes are available too. Honey roasted Kelmscott ham served with egg and chips is a firm favourite and the Gloucestershire old spot sausages and mash served with caramelised red onions and a red wine gravy are scrumptious. In fact, I like this unspoiled pub so much that I regularly use it as a lunch venue if I am meeting up with friends.

The Walk

As this area has many footpaths there are several walks you can take on leaving the pub.

We arrived half an hour before the pub opened for lunch one day, so used the time to enjoy a delightful little walk by following the footpath sign to Shipton-on-Cherwell, found on your left if you are facing the pub. This mile-long walk begins by following the lane until a stile that takes you onto a green lane. At this point the canal is on your right hand side, hidden partly from view by a line of mature trees.

There's not much more you need to know after that as the lane continues through a newly planted woodland. During what proves to be a circular walk, you will encounter a couple of notices stating that walkers are welcome by agreement of the owner, who is cultivating the

Pythius says

Every now and again Auntie Liz and Helen actually get it right and find me a walk that allows me to really have fun. When they manage to find two quite different walks on the same day, a river and a dog-friendly pub too – what can I say except thank you?

The remarkable thing about these walks is that they didn't get lost once. We didn't even have to make a return trip another day to check whether walkers should turn left or right when they get to a certain point. (I won't admit just how many times that happens, but be assured it does – and often – as they are usually chattering so much they forget to notice where we are going).

The Boat is quite delightful, just what you would expect of a little country pub that stands by the canal. I like it because it attracts a lot of boatmen and holidaymakers who seem to take kindly to dogs such as me. Conversations with them are frequent. The licensee is a kindly man too. He wrapped up some of Auntie Liz's fish for me one day because she couldn't eat it all. Nice gesture that! It would have been even nicer if Helen had allowed me to eat it there and then – but she didn't.

I admit to liking the river walk best as I am able to romp around in wild grasses and jump in and out of the river when we take that path. But the new woodland walk was great too: Loads of space to run about, no cows to worry about, just grass and trees of all shapes and sizes, then a big field. No dog could possibly ask for more.

woodland for our enjoyment with the help of the Forestry Commission. Half way round the woodland, you will come to a metal gate that leads to the road. Here you will find a footpath sign which sends you round the edge of a large field and back to the pub.

The second walk is quite different as it takes you along the canal and on to the River Cherwell and the many mature trees that line its banks.

With your back to the pub, turn left and then left again, following the line of attractive little cottages alongside the canal. A small bridge spanning the canal leads to Annie's Tea Rooms on the left and a lane which leads to small tunnel that passes under the railway line. Just beyond the tunnel, you reach a small wooden gate and discover the Thrupp Community Woodlands map mounted on the left-hand side.

I don't need to tell you much more. One look at the map will show you the many footpaths that run alongside the river or zigzag through the woodlands to Kidlington's parish church of St Mary the Virgin. Follow the river path and you will eventually arrive at Hampton Poyle and the Bell Inn, about a mile away and another fantastic dog-friendly pub which serves great meals and where you could stop for refreshments before returning to Thrupp.

Or you can do what we normally do, which is to amble for about half a mile along the winding river bank, admiring all the wild flowers that flourish in this unspoiled place, until you come to a shallow bay. It's here that the dog can have great fun splashing around to his heart's delight in reasonably shallow clean water.

Then, when you have exhausted the dog, return the way you came, popping

into Annie's for a cup of tea and a slice of home-made cake, which you can enjoy sitting at the tables set up outside the café, before going home.

History

There was a moment in the Boat's history which was not so jolly. On Christmas Eve 1874, this pub was one of many buildings in the area that took in injured passengers when a train bound for the Midlands plunged down the embankment beside the canal. A wheel had broken on the extra coach that had been added to accommodate the large number of travellers who embarked at Oxford. Thirty passengers died in the crash as the coaches slipped beneath the canal's icy water that snowy night just before the nearby station at Shipton-on-Cherwell, and more than 70 were injured, making it the worst train crash in railway history. Even Queen Victoria was moved to send a message of sympathy.

Wantage
The Lamb Inn

The Lamb Inn, Mill Street, Wantage, is a 17th century thatched pub that stands close to Wessex Mill at the edge of this bustling little market town, and close to the John Betjeman Memorial Park.

Actually we not only chose this pub because it is dog-friendly but because it is close to this lovely little park which celebrates the fact that John Betjeman has strong links with the town. Unfortunately we soon discovered that dogs (even on a lead) are not permitted in the park – yet litter-louts are, judging by the empty beer cans and crisp packets.

We were unaware of this as we sipped our glasses of Fuller's London Pride, spending some time reading the little jokes written boldly on the beams decorating this pub, of which there are many.

This pub was renovated and enlarged during the 20th century, giving it a modern feel and loads of space for mothers with their prams and the many people like us who arrive with their dogs.

The menu offers something for everyone, with light bites like crispy-coated vegetables, breaded camembert and steaming dishes of soup.

Because it attracts people of all ages, this pub is a very happy place, where some people come to gossip and others because they need lunch. Pythius was certainly made welcome.

The Walk

Oh dear, Uncle John and I had intended to walk round the John Betjeman Memorial Park, admire the statue of the poet, and read some of his better known works on display. Instead we had to take the lane from the pub car park that runs alongside the park and follows Letcombe Brook for a short way until we reached the Mill House and a ford. This only took about ten minutes.

Fortunately the water in the ford kept Pythius amused for some considerable time, such that he was quite happy to turn right into Locks Lane, then right again into Priory Road and back towards the centre of town. Once in the Market Square you can admire King Alfred's imposing statue that stands in the centre.

For those looking for a long walk, or a space where dogs can run free, this is not for them. But if you are happy to trot round this remarkable little town, weaving through its streets and lanes soaking up its historic atmosphere, you are assured of a jolly and informative time.

One very positive thing about this walk is the friendly way residents greet visitors. During our saunter round Wantage, several struck up conversations with us and everyone we approached for directions took the trouble to explain what we should look out for along the way.

History

King Alfred the Great has become a symbol of Wantage as he was born here in 849. His royal Saxon residence is thought to have been somewhere between Letcombe Brook and Grove Street.

His statue was donated to the town by Col. Robert Loyd-Lindsay and unveiled by the Prince and Princess of Wales on 14 July 1877. In January 2008 the statue was vandalised. Alfred's right arm which brandished a battle axe was cut off and smashed. It has been repaired and King Alfred now stands proud and whole again.

Pythius Says

They promised me a walk in the park, but this didn't happen. When we got to the gates of the park, there it was, that dreaded notice that has spoiled so many dog days out. NO DOGS.

I have seen it so many times, I have come to recognise the letters that make up these words and accept the inevitable – no dogs. Therefore no fun!

Actually it was OK, Helen was so upset at seeing this notice that she allowed me to splash and splash and splash in the ford at the bottom of the lane, so that I could use up some of my excess energy. Credit where credit is due, she does try to keep me happy when we are out together and things begin to go pear-shaped.

Walking round the town was quite nice because the people were so friendly. Several made admiring noises as I walked past them and one nice lady actually patted me on the head.

Warborough
Six Bells

The moment I parked the car outside the Six Bells, Warborough, Auntie Liz looked round at the village green, and declared this must be a Midsomer Murders location. She was right. Over the years, Warborough has provided the backdrop for several episodes of the popular ITV detective series starring John Nettles.

I asked her how she knew this. She explained that the village green, cricket pavilion and village pub simply cried out to be used for a murder mystery television series. Looking round at the assorted thatched cottages and quaint houses that flanked the green, I had to agree. Warborough is as quintessentially English as the television films in which it has featured. It lies three miles north of Wallingford.

The Six Bells, named when six bells were rehung in the village church of St Laurence in the 1900s, is the sort of English pub you dream of visiting. Not only does it boast a thatched roof and stand besides the village green, it oozes with atmosphere. The beamed ceilings are low, the beams are gnarled, and the log fires that are lit in the winter add a dancing warmth to this superb pub with its many intimate rooms and spaces. I have visited the Six Bells frequently and have never been disappointed.

Pythius says

Well, all I can say about the Six Bells is that it is a fantastic pub, which made me feel like royalty when I entered. The staff were so kind to me and several customers, including a really nice Australian couple, patted me on the head and made me feel really important. Border collies do like to be noticed and they certainly noticed me.

As for the walk, well it was a relief to be on a walk that was so easy to follow that Helen and Auntie Liz didn't get lost. We went round in a circle, but it was a really nice circle, that followed the perimeter of the fields and ended up back at the village green. Yes, I accept that there was that moment when I decided to jump into the drainage ditch; well, why not? It was all muddy and gooey and for the few glorious moments I was able to roll about in that sticky muck at the bottom. I did have a wonderful time. The fact that I emerged looking brown rather than black and white didn't bother me too much. I have no idea why the girls made such a fuss! I guess I have to accept that there are times when the things that please me just don't please them!

It's a Brakspear pub, so a good selection of real ales brewed in Oxfordshire is assured, and the food, which is cooked to order, follows the seasons. What more could anyone ask for?

When we arrived with Pythius, we were made welcome and offered a comfortable place in the bar area. Bowls of water for visiting canines stand outside the front door. We could have sat in the attractive pub garden, but Pythius enjoys a pub atmosphere, so we remained inside.

The service here is second to none. Customers are treated like kings and queens. Orders are taken at the table, including drinks orders, which are professionally delivered with a smile. In other words, once you have arrived and settled at a table, you can relax and enjoy the luxury of being looked after by a professional team who appear hell bent on making your visit enjoyable.

When I asked where we could take Pythius for a walk once we had finished our lunch, we were told that the area was riddled with footpaths, and that if we walked through the village green, which is the largest green in Oxfordshire, we would find ourselves in deep country which our dog would love. They were right – he did.

The Walk

This walk couldn't be easier. All you do is turn right out of the pub, walk down the village green until you meet a tarmac road to the right which takes you on a circular walk. You will notice after walking for a short while that you can join a green path that runs parallel to the road and alongside the field on your right. This eventually turns back into the tarmac road which leads to a path alongside a wheat field on the left. Here you will discover a drainage ditch full of sturdy bulrushes – and lots of mud.

Unfortunately Pythius noticed the mud before we did, and he dived in, only to emerge covered with the brown stuff. And when I say covered, I really do mean covered. Any remnants of white fur which would have distinguished him as a border collie had vanished. We had a dirty, smelly *brown* dog on our hands! The path along this field finally opens out to a green lane, and a sign pointing the way we had come which indicates we had just taken a millennium walk on a permissive footpath which can only be used by owner's consent. The green lane, which leads back to the village green, is a delight. The hedgerows are filled with a fine assortment of plants, including sloes and hawthorn. All you do now is walk straight, passing the well-kept village allotments along the way.

Because we ambled, it took us about an hour to complete the circle, but walkers striding out at a fair pace could have walked the circle in half the time. This is flat open country, offering views of the historic Wittenham Clumps in the far distance. The only strange thing about this walk, which we did just a few days after visiting Juniper Hill, was the lack of wildlife and butterflies. Our Juniper Hill walk had proved a real delight, offering an abundance of butterflies. There were very few butterflies at Warborough, despite the many wild flowers we discovered, and I have no idea why.

History

During the summers of 1844-45 Joseph Tubb, from Warborough, carved the poem that can still be seen on the Poem Tree, to be found on Castle Hill, Wittenham Clumps.

Although the tree on which the poem was carved has now died, some of the trunk is still standing and

cuts made by his knife can still be seen in the bark. Thanks to Dr Henry Osmaston, who took a tracing of the poem in 1965 when it was much more legible, a plaque reproducing the tracing can be seen standing next to the tree. (See p92 for further comments on this historic tree, which we visited when climbing the Clumps).

West Hanney
The Plough

The first time that Pythius and I enjoyed lunch at The Plough, West Hanney, was unplanned. I intended to drive further afield, but the newly-thatched Plough Inn, with its whitewashed walls and ornamental redbrick trim, looked so inviting, my faithful old Mini ground to a halt the moment it came into view. I found myself steering it into the car park opposite without a second thought.

For those seeking a quintessential English pub this is one, and what's more dogs are very welcome in the bar area.

West Hanney, which is just two miles north of Wantage, was placed firmly in Berkshire until 1974 when the boundaries were changed and it woke one morning to discover it had become an Oxfordshire pub.

To get to West Hanney you first have to travel through East Hanney. If you approach from the A338, just a field separates the two villages which both date back to pre Norman times. On West Hanney's western boundary stands what is left of the deserted medieval village of North Denchworth.

Letcombe Brook runs through the villages. Until 1920 the brook provided power to several mills which are disused now.

Well, that's the history done with, let's talk about the pub now – because this really is a special place which is professionally run and is one of those friendly pubs that makes you feel good about yourself the moment you walk through the door.

Two special friends Judy and Wanda and their dear old dog Toby joined me on my last visit as they live nearby. It's one of their favourite pubs too, especially as Toby is allowed to join them.

We called on a Thursday, which meant that anyone with a pensioner's card can eat a superb meal at a much reduced price. We all ordered the roast of the day, which proved half the price we would have paid  anywhere else for a home cooked meal, with real crunchy roast potatoes and fresh seasonal vegetables. It was so good that a silence descended at our table until every scrap had been finished. The standard menu offers loads of delicious home-cooked dishes created from local produce. As Dews Meadow Farm Shop is a couple of miles away, pork, bacon and sausages seldom travel more than a mile or so from farm to plate – you can't get much more local than that.

On the day we called Trevor and Ann Cooper, who have run the pub for several years, were thrilled to inform us that it will soon be a free house. Whilst they will still continue serving real ales such as Timothy Taylor's Landlord, they plan to serve several local brews too.

When Trevor learned that Pythius is a member of CAMRA he was most impressed and was about to offer him a bowl of ale, until I assured him Pythius would stick to water and just enjoy the aroma of malt that wafted under the table from our drinks.

The Walk

The walk couldn't be easier and it is another of those walks that can be as long or as short as you would like it to be.

On leaving the pub, cross the road and turn left towards the church of St James the Great, which stands on a Saxon site and dates back to Norman times. Spend a moment admiring the inner arch of the north porch, which is an excellent example of Norman carving of a chevron pattern supported by twisted shafts and finely carved capitals. The font is worth a few moments of your time too, as it dates back to the Norman period and is beautifully carved with delicate vertical bands of rosettes.

Pythius says

I still remember the first time Helen spotted this pub, I thought she had crashed the car because it stopped so suddenly. "Look at that Pythius! Gosh, we have to go in there!" she declared in one of those excited voices she uses from time to time. I wanted to remind her we were headed for a pub further afield, but when she makes up her mind, there is no arguing with her, so I just accepted her spontaneity and went with the flow. In fact she was so excited, that for one dreadful moment I thought she would forget to take me with her!

Of course she was right to be excited – she has a nose for good pubs, I always trust her instinct. She says it is something to do with the total look of the pub, the way it is kept, the hanging baskets and all those sort of things. I remember once she even judged a pub by its clean dustbins, which she kept staring at in wonder as if she had never seen a dustbin before. Anyway – she was right. The pub was great. I was made welcome, she enjoyed her meal and real ale and everyone was happy.

I must admit that when she gets together with Judy and Wanda, as we did recently, they all chatter so much I am often forgotten. They are usually discussing the Island Farm Donkey Sanctuary, that they are involved with, and have so much to say about the poor distressed donkeys that they help to get well again. When I hear the plight of some of the donkeys they care for, it makes me realise that we animals owe a great deal to kind people like Wanda and Judy who really care about how we are treated.

The walk was fine, after what I considered a boring moment or two inspecting the church, it was just a trip through the churchyard, a couple of gates and my lead was slipped off and I was free to roam. So was dear old Toby, who didn't think much of stopping off to view a church either, for despite great age, this dear little dog still loves roaming free and sniffing the surroundings. We didn't walk too fast, as Toby is getting on: he has problems with his hearing too, which means I was asked to keep an eye on him in case he got lost.

Unfortunately I had barked at him once several years ago for no real reason, and bless him he has always remembered that and been rather cautious in my company. This time, I decided to sort this out and had a long chat with him as we walked. I even apologised for my bad temper when we last met. Being the kindly old man he is, he accepted my apology and we then got on really well. He didn't get lost once. In fact we both had a lovely time weaving in and out of the trees and plodding through the long grasses.

The walk starts at the back of the churchyard, so make your way round the church, bearing to the left at the bottom until you reach a wooden kissing gate, turn right, walk a few more yards and you will encounter another wooden gate named The Tyser Gate. A yellow waymarker points the way to the community woodlands planted about 15 years ago by the kindly farmer from Church Farm.

At this point you can either walk backwards and forwards through the avenues of trees which will delight the dog, or march straight ahead, turning right when you spot a division in the well-maintained green pathways. Keep walking and you will eventually come to another gate and yellow way sign. Once through the gate you can turn sharp right again through a hole in the foliage, and then fight your way through a tangle of undergrowth and low branches of young trees and keep walking along a faintly defined pathway beside a field.

This will eventually lead you to a stone track. Or, having turned left after passing through the gate, keep going along the side of a large field until you meet up with the track.

To turn this into a circular walk, you now turn right and follow the track past the farmyard and back to the pub. You come out just a few yards from The Plough. A footpath sign the other side of the road might look inviting if you feel you want to walk further, but this only leads to another road in the village and is not very exciting for dogs. We ambled and explored the woodlands for a while so the walk took us about an hour. It's up to you to design the walk to suit your needs.

History

For those who enjoy quirky historical facts, the Hanneys claim that the oldest ever recorded English woman, Elizabeth Bowles, lived in the area. She is said to have died in 1718 at the grand old age of 124. A plaque on the front of the north wall of the church boasts this fact. The secret of her longevity has never been disclosed.

Sadly The Plough certainly can't claim her long life was due to its beer, for although the building dates back to 1525, it has only been operating as a pub for about 180 years. It was built at a time when Henry VIII built the nearby Dower House for one of his many mistresses, and four cottages for the workers.

West Hendred
The Hare

Every year Pythius gets given a shampoo so that he looks smart for the annual Animal Blessing Service, which he has been attending since he was a puppy. The service, which is organised by my two special friends Wanda and Judy, takes place at St John Vianney Church, Wantage. Any money collected at the service goes towards the upkeep of the Island Farm Donkey Sanctuary at Brightwell-cum-Sotwell, near Wallingford. This service is such fun as so many different animals are brought in for a blessing. Even hens, rabbits and guinea pigs attend with their owners. But first we have a pub lunch, then take Pythius for a long walk so that he will be relaxed during the service.

The Hare, West Hendred, is our usual choice as this bustling little pub is just a couple of miles from Wantage on the Reading Road (A417). You can't miss it because this whitewashed, wood-clad pub looks rather like a colonial building, and stands next to the bus stop and opposite the little road leading to the main village of West Hendred and Ginge.

A large stone lion sits somnolently besides one of the pillars. The bar and restaurant areas are as attractive as the exterior, and the wooden theme dominates throughout.

The Sunday lunch that this friendly pub serves is so good and so reasonably priced, I doubt I'd bother to cook a roast at home if I lived in the area. This is due in part to the fact the licensee was once a butcher; the meat served here is always succulent. The selection of fresh seasonal vegetables offered with a roast lunch is so generous we usually struggle to eat them all. The crunchy roast potatoes and roast parsnips are to die for.

As Sunday lunch is served throughout the day, this pub is well worth a visit, particularly as they serve a great selection of well-kept real ale too. Pythius was made very welcome, as The Hare is a pub that accepts dogs in the bar area. He needed a bowl of water, and it arrived promptly in a posh stainless steel dog bowl. What dog could ask for more? As the footpath that will take the walker all the way to Steventon is right next door to the pub, it offers everything a dog owner could wish for too.

The Walk

As you leave the pub you will discover a green lane on the right hand side which is marked as a footpath. There is also a bridle-way about 30 yards left of the pub which goes in the same direction. If you take the bridle-way, you will have to cross the road and walk the distance on the pathway provided, as the A417 is a very busy road and there is no path on the left hand side.

We take the footpath right next to the pub, which leads to a metal gate. There's no need to climb the gate as a well walked gap beside the

---

Pythius says

If I didn't have to suffer the indignity of a bath before going to the annual Blessing service, perhaps I would really enjoy this event. Sitting in a church among animals of all shapes and sizes is certainly fun, especially when it comes to the hymns – even the chickens get excited when everyone sings All Things Bright and Beautiful. Sometimes Pollyanne the donkey joins in too.

Helen always calls the Blessing my insurance for the year. I'm not sure what this means, but attending the service seems to be important to her – so who am I to argue? The pub down the road is lovely; nice cool floors and very kind waiting staff, who always bring me a posh bowl of water when I need it. Lots of dogs use this pub, and then take their masters for a walk afterwards.

The walk is fine because we always walk this way during the autumn when the fields have been ploughed. During the summer months they are usually filled with crops and I have to keep to the path at all times. The badger holes are certainly worth inspecting, they are big and gloriously smelly. In fact, they are so big Helen gets quite anxious if I try to climb down into the holes and explore. We have to be very careful when we get to the end of this walk and approach the road; this is where Helen puts me on a tight lead as the traffic moves at speed.

gate offers enough space for everyone to walk through. Because the fields adjoining this walk are enormous, you will immediately be struck by the feeling of space that this walk offers. Look up and you will be entertained by red kites soaring overhead. Look down and in places you will encounter large badger setts and an abundance of wild flowers.

After walking the length of one field you will come to an overgrown lane which was once passable, but is now a tangle of hawthorn and weeds. At this point turn into the field on your right and either circum-navigate this field (as we did) picking up the bridle-way when you have done the entire circuit and following that back to the A417. This will

give you a walk of approximately a mile, but you can keep going left following the well marked bridle-way to Steventon, which is about two miles away.

History

West Hendred's close proximity to Wantage suggests that there's every chance that King Alfred would have trod the earth in this area.

And if you want a quirky piece of history: This area is thought to be haunted by a man killed in a road accident. The ghost was first sighted by two sisters driving through the village at night who encountered a man wearing a cap and overcoat rushing in front of their car. The driver braked and waited for the crash as the car hit the man, but they experienced nothing, the road was empty and the man had vanished.

The Hare and Hounds Westonbirt

The Hare and Hounds which stands next to Westonbirt, the national arboretum, on the A433 near Tetbury, exemplifies my theory that stylish pubs are often more dog-friendly than scruffy ones.

Uncle John and I had driven past the Hare and Hounds on our way to Westonbirt, and promised ourselves that we would check it out after our trip to the arboretum.

When I walked into Jack Hare's Bar to check that Pythius would be welcome, the barman looked puzzled – surely this was a question that didn't need asking. Of course they were welcome, he assured me.

Pythius trotted in head held high, made his way to a corner table by the window and settled himself until we had finished our meal. It was all very friendly and companionable, despite the fact that this is a very chic hotel – dare I say posh?

A superb mural of beagles dominates the back of the bar, log fires are lit during the cold months, and the staff are both efficient and friendly.

The bar menu, which is available throughout the day, offers a great assortment of meals, and whilst dishes such as fillet steak with all the trimmings were highly priced, the sandwiches which we ordered were very reasonable and tasted absolutely delicious. Uncle John was

Pythius says

What a walk! Gosh I did enjoy myself. A real social event actually, as there were almost as many dogs walking through the trees as people. So many fantastic smells too as each visiting dog had left its mark, which of course had to be inspected. No self-respecting dog can walk past an interesting scent without investigating it.

Helen and Uncle John were so absorbed by everything around them that they didn't seem to mind me wandering off now and again to check the dog-messages that were clinging to the base of the trees.

Then there were all those dogs to talk to: big dogs, little dogs, poodle type dogs with bows in their hair, and even a few Border Collies like me, all being terribly sociable. What fun I had.

The pub was really nice too, so friendly. As Helen said it was very stylish, loads of little rooms adjoining the bar where we could eat. I chose one in the front near the window, but could have easily tucked myself in a corner of one of the other little rooms. No one seemed to mind where we sat.

Naturally I slept all the way home.

---

particularly impressed when he noticed that we had been served one and a half rounds of sandwiches, a generous leaf salad, and a mountain of crisps. He agreed that we have often paid far more for less at other pubs along the way and munched down his lunch with relish.

Champagne appeared to be the house wine, but there's an extensive selection of real ales too. A quick glance around the room assured me that we were not the only beer drinkers that lunchtime.

Should you call on a sunny day there's an attractive little beer garden outside.

Because this lovely hotel has been owned by the same family for more than 50 years, and is set amid beautiful gardens and woodland, a visit here combined with a trip to Westonbirt Arboretum offers the perfect day out. Pythius certainly enjoyed himself.

The Walk

As autumn is the high point of the Westonbirt year and the time when the arboretum is ablaze with colour, we made our visit during mid-October. Visit Westonbirt's website and you will discover an entire page dedicated to dogs, as this is one of those glorious places where dogs are welcome. Only the Old Arboretum, the restaurant, shop, toilets and the Great Oak Hall are designated dog-free areas. Toilets were put out of bounds when staff discovered dogs had been given a bath in the washbasins on a muddy day! I smiled at the thought of trying to lift Pythius into a hand basin and give him a wash – memories of that fateful day I tried to wash him in the bath flooded back. Some of the mud he shook off that day still stains the ceiling and I never managed to get the towel really clean again.

There's no need to give directions for this walk. All you do, having paid the modest entrance fee and parked the car, is to pick up a free guide and make for the dog area, which is clearly marked as Silk Wood.

On our visit, this was easy, everyone appeared to be accompanied by at least one dog, so it was just a matter of following the crowd, which thins out immediately you have entered the gate, allowing walkers to choose the avenue they wish to explore.

We were impressed to discover that free dog-bags complete with handles were readily available from a dispenser by the entrance to enable owners to remove dog mess with ease if they have forgotten to bring a plastic bag with them.

Pythius had the most wonderful time picking up all the dog scents, while we walked quiet paths set in woodland dating from the 13th century and admired the glorious autumnal colours of the trees. The

Japanese Maples were the prima donnas of the collection while we were there.

Actually it proved a mind-blowing experience, particularly as we were able to walk the stately avenues and trails for as long as we liked. I guess we covered at least two miles, wandering freely between the trees, before deciding it was time for lunch. We could have walked more had we wished. Pythius probably walked twice that amount and was exhausted by the time we had returned to the car. Yes, of course we took loads of photographs during our walk, but the magical thing about this place is that the best images I have of those fabulous trees remain in my head.

History

Westonbirt Arboretum was founded in 1829 and is now of one of the world's largest, with more than 18,000 trees in its 600 acres of Grade 1 listed landscape. The Forestry Commission acquired the arboretum in 1956 and has maintained and extended it ever since as a collection for scientific and educational purposes, as well as for the enjoyment of the public.

Woodstock
The Bear

Y ou can't miss the Bear Hotel if you visit the historic town of Woodstock. It stands bang in the centre of town, right next to the Market Square. This beautiful ivy-clad hotel, which began life as a 13th-century coaching inn, is one of Pythius' favourite places.

He first walked the creaking stairs to the top floor when making his way to the temporary green room, reserved for authors during Woodstock's annual literary festival (Yes, he was invited to take part in the Festival in 2009 and it rather went to his head). Ever since that moment, he has always pulled on the lead if we pass the Bear, in the hope that he can settle his paws under the table in the lovely little bar on the right hand side of the entrance where well mannered dogs are made welcome.

If I tell you this is the hotel where Richard Burton and Elizabeth Taylor stayed at the height of their passionate love affair, when they appeared together at the Oxford Playhouse, you will appreciate that this is hostelry of distinction. This means of course that even a humble pint of beer and a sandwich will be costly. That said, drink orders are served by a waiter who brings everything to the table on a tray lined with a linen napkin, and who bows subserviently when dispensing the order. Pythius's request for water arrived in a posh pink doggie bowl filled to the brim with iced water which was served with the same deference as my beer.

In the winter, the roaring log fire adds its own atmospheric touch, such that visitors are reluctant to leave the comfortable leather chairs that furnish this historic little room. Unfortunately the choice of beers is not impressive, but I usually find that there's at least one real ale on tap.

We normally begin a walk round Blenheim Palace grounds by calling in at the Bear for a beer, and then finish our walk by visiting Harriet's

Pythius says

I must be getting old, because I am about to admit I don't mind being kept on my lead when visiting Woodstock, the Bear and Harriet's Tea Rooms. There is something quite magical about this town, especially if a visit to the palace grounds is included. We sometimes visit the Woodstock Bookshop too, where I am always greeted warmly by a lovely woman called Rachel, and where my previous book is sometimes displayed in the window.

The Bear is simply amazing. I am bowed in as if I am a star, and the pink water bowl is placed gently beside me as if I am a really important guest. I like that. I also like it when I am bowed out by a member of staff who just happens to be standing close to the main door when I leave.

As for the walk, well what can I say? It is spectacular. Obviously I find it frustrating when I see all that water, yet know I am not going to be allowed to splash about. But the ducks, moorhens, swans and Canada geese keep me amused with their antics as they bob about on the water. Kestrels flying over-head are worth watching too.

Naturally Helen clutches a plastic bag while we walk this park, just in case I let her down, but so far I have never done so.

Tea at Harriet's afterwards is great fun too, particularly as I am offered a doggie treat by Judy, the kindly proprietor, as soon as I have settled my paws under the table.

Yes, a visit to the palace is always great fun. I certainly prefer walking though the palace grounds to taking that lane the other side of town, past the cemetery, where the litter I mentioned in my previous book still lingers.

Cake Shop just down the road for afternoon tea where the prices are more realistic and the food is scrumptious. It's here that Pythius is offered a treat the moment he walks in, as this is one of those rare tea shops where dogs are welcome providing they behave themselves.

If you follow our lead and visit Harriet's, which was built in 1627, do take a moment to admire the many decorative carved timbers around the door frames and windows. They were taken from the great galleons of the Spanish Armada and have been preserved so well they look like modern carvings.

The Walk

You have several choices when walking the grounds of Blenheim Palace – you can drive into the main gate and dutifully pay your entrance fee, which gives you access to the palace, or do what the locals do, which is to enter by a side gate for free on one of the several rights of way that cross the park and are marked on Ordnance Survey maps.

Free entrance means you have to walk in an anti-clockwise direction round the lake without stopping off to visit the palace or many of the special gardens. But, if like us, you simply want to soak up the atmosphere of this great place, admire the work of Capability Brown who landscaped this 2,000-acre park, and enjoy a circular walk around the lake, then go for the side gate.

When you first approach this gate, which is found on the A44 leading out of Woodstock towards Chipping Norton, and almost opposite the Black Horse pub, you will probably walk straight past, assuming it is the entrance to a private house. But don't be fooled by the number 95 pinned on this green gate, as it really does lead to a short passage way and another green gate opening out into the palace grounds.

Open that second gate and you will find yourself in wonderland. Regardless of the season, you will be surrounded with beauty, as Capability Brown's main aim was to give the spectator the idea that the suave, sweeping beauty of the parks he created in the 18th century was the result of happy accidents of nature. Not for him the geometric patterns and classical temples found in other parks of this period. He planted many

of the trees in clumps and designed water features and lakes that looked as if they had been there since the beginning of time.

The result is a breathtaking landscape that never ceases to delight. Even Pythius seems overawed when we walk through that green gate.

He has to remain on the lead, but for some reason I have never understood, he seems to accept this when we walk round the lake at Blenheim.

Circling the lake will take you about an hour if you amble, taking time to admire yet another view, another ancient tree, another vista. There are many other possibilities for longer walks on rights of way within the park, or by picking up the Oxfordshire Way where it follows the line of Roman Akeman Street through the northern tip of the park near Ditchley Gate.

Pythius and I last walked the palace grounds in the autumn with both Auntie Liz and Uncle John when the glorious autumn colours were at their height. I don't think I have ever seen anything more beautiful.

History

Blenheim Palace, which is now owned by the 11th Duke of Marlborough, was built in 1715 by the architect Sir John Vanbrugh, and landscaped by Lancelot 'Capability' Brown, who is said to have planned the avenues and trees to represent a plan of the Battle of Blenheim. Some of the oaks that remain standing after the great storm of 1987 go back to the time of the Plantagenet kings.

Pythius-Peacocke's last word

Well, that's it then, more pubs, more walks and all of them woven into the thousands of years of history that made our landscape what it is today.

Once again I have been taken to some superb pubs and enjoyed fabulous country walks that all dogs should experience at least once a week.

Just occasionally things went slightly pear-shaped – the Wantage walk for instance does not rate among my favourites as we encountered that dreaded sign NO DOGS as soon as we approached the entrance to the John Betjeman Memorial Park – but that sort of thing didn't happen often. Most walks that I took with Helen, Auntie Liz, Uncle John, Auntie Kate and my other friends were filled with fun, water, space and lots and lots of lovely fresh air. The fact that it rained and I got covered with mud sometimes didn't really matter, Helen's old Mini is so scruffy that any dirt I deposit on the back seat simply adds to its rustic interior.

Of course there were times when Helen got really cross with me, particularly if I rolled in a lovely foxy smell, or trod in a juicy cowpat, but such moments pass and all is finally forgiven.

My aim when helping her write this book was to encourage dog owners to consider – when planning a day out – enjoying a pub lunch in a dog-friendly pub, followed by a brisk walk through the country-side. Such adventures help cement that special bond between dog and owner. They also bring extra trade to atmospheric country pubs that deserve to remain open, but which may be struggling with the adverse effects of the recession.

More than 30 pubs are still closing each week nationwide – so it really is a matter of using them or losing them. I vote for using them.

Some of the real ales we enjoyed along the way

The real ales we have encountered during our travels always add an extra flavour-dimension to the day. It's the thought of a foaming glass of local ale that has kept us going during many a long walk.

Because today's breweries follow the seasons, brewing spicy, ruby-rich ales during the winter months, and golden thirst-quenching summer brews during warmer times, we have never been disappointed. Here are a few of my favourite tipples.

Best Mates Brewery Ltd

Founded in 2007 on the Lockinge Estate, near Wantage, this micro-brewery takes its water from a local bore hole on the estate, which is so crisp and pure that their beers are certainly worth trying.

Try Alfie's (4.4% ABV), named after England's 9th monarch, born just a stone's throw from the brewery, which is spiced with coriander.

The Cotswold Brewing Company

Situated in an old Cotswold stone farm building, this brewery produces lagers from the purest products and without the use of preservatives.

Cotswold Premium Lager (5% ABV) is by far their biggest seller and for good reason. It's a full-flavoured brew with a crisp, dry taste that comes with a bitter kick.

Donnington Brewery

This Gloucestershire brewery established in 1865 produces beers from the recipes which originated more than 150 years ago and uses water drawn from a spring beside the brewery's mill pond, as it did when the brewery was founded.

Its S.B.A. (4.4% ABV) is a great brew as malt dominates over bitterness, producing subtle flavours that come with a hint of fruit and a dry, malty finish.

Hook Norton Brewery Co.Ltd

This family-owned Victorian brewery, which was established 150 years ago and still relies on steam power to pump the water to drive the

grist mill, has come up with some amazing award-winning real ales over the years.

My favourite is Old Hooky (4.6% ABV) which is a beautifully balanced beer with a well-rounded body, which satisfies one's taste buds throughout the year.

Wychwood Brewery

This enterprising little brewery, established in 1983 and situated in the centre of Witney, is named after the ancient forest of Wychwood.

The names of many of its brews reflect this fact.

In July 2004, Wychwood took over the production of the Henley based Brakspear Brewery which dated back to 1711. This was apt given that Robert Brakspear actually began his brewing career in the Cross Keys pub, Witney. For those interested in quirky historical facts, a distant ancestor of Robert Brakspear was Britain's only pope. Nicholas Breakspear ruled as Pope Adrian the Fourth from 1154 to 1159.

Hobgoblin (4.5% ABV) is Wychwood's flagship beer and for good reason; this ruby-coloured full-bodied beer has a delicious chocolate toffee malt flavour which keeps you asking for more.

Brakspear's Oxford Gold Organic Beer (4% ABV) with its fresh, citrus aromas and firm, fruity flavour is a fine example of how a brewery can come up with a new brew that hits the spot every time. Certainly a beer I order without hesitation when it's on tap.

Pub contact information

Abingdon   The Old Anchor Inn 01235 521 762

Adderbury   The Bell 01295 810 338
                www.thebell-adderbury.com

Ampney Crucis   The Crown of Crucis 01285 851806
                    www.thecrownofcrucis.co.uk

Ardington   The Boar's Head 01235 833 254
                www.boarsheadardington.co.uk

Cassington   The Chequers 01865
                www.chequres-inn-cassington.co.uk

Chedworth   Seven Tuns 01285 720 242

Cropredy   The Red Lion 01295 750 224
                www.redlioncroperdy.com

Cumnor   The Bear and ragged Staff 01865 862329
                www.bearandraggedstaff-cumnor.com

Deddington   The Unicorn Inn 01869 338 838
                www.theunicorninn.net

Dorchester-on-Thames   Fleur de Lys 01865 340 502
                           www.fleurdelys-dorchester.co.uk

Eaton   The Eight Bells 01865 865 389

Edge Hill   Castle Inn 01295 670 255

Enstone   The Crown 01993 868 431

Eynsham   The Red Lion 01865 882 903

Fairford   The Bull Hotel 01285 712 535
                www.thebullhotelfairford.co.uk

Fringford   The Butcher's Arms 01869 277 363

Hailey   The Lamb and Flag 01993 702 849

Hook Norton   The Pear Tree Inn 01608 737 482

Islip   The Swan 01865 372 590
                       www.swan-islip.co.uk/

Long Wittenham   The Plough Inn 01865 407 738

Longworth   The Blue Boar 01865 820 494
                       www.blueboarlongworth.co.uk

Northmoor   The Red Lion 01865 521 033
                       www.redlionnorthmoor.com

Oxford (Botley)   The George 01865 244 795

Oxford (Walton Manor) The Anchor Inn 01865 510 282
                       www.theanchoroxford.com

Quenington   The Keepers Arms 01285 750 349
                       www.thekeepersarms.co.uk

Southrop   The Swan 01367 850 205
                       www.theswansouthrop.co.uk

Stoke Row   The Cherry Tree Inn 01491 680 430
                       www.thecherrytreeinn.com

Sutton Courtenay   The George and Dragon 08721 077077

Thrupp   The Boat Inn 01865 374 279
                       www.theboatinnthrupp.co.uk

Wantage   The Lamb Inn   01235 766 768

Warborough   Six Bells 01865 858 265
                       www.sixbellswarborough.com

West Hanney   The Plough 01235 868 674
                       www.plough-westhanney.co.uk

West Hendred   The Hare 01235 833 249
                       www.thehairathendred.co.uk

Westonbirt   Hare and Hounds 01666 880 233
                       www.bw-hare-hounds-wetonbirt.htm

Woodstock   The Bear 0844 879 9143
                       www.macdonaldhotels.co.uk/bear

Quote

If dogs were asked what they thought of history, they would say it didn't rate that highly on the list of things they love the most.

And if asked what they dreamed of, they would lick their lips and speak of food – but not any kind of food.

Most would request their own personal chef, able to cook up steaming dishes of pheasant stew, rabbit pie and a few other tasty dishes created just for them.

They know it won't happen – but dogs are allowed their dreams too.

Anon